S. HRG. 113–522

# WHEN CATASTROPHE STRIKES: RESPONSES TO NATURAL DISASTERS IN INDIAN COUNTRY

# HEARING

BEFORE THE

## COMMITTEE ON INDIAN AFFAIRS
## UNITED STATES SENATE

ONE HUNDRED THIRTEENTH CONGRESS

SECOND SESSION

JULY 30, 2014

Printed for the use of the Committee on Indian Affairs

U.S. GOVERNMENT PRINTING OFFICE

92–272 PDF        WASHINGTON : 2015

For sale by the Superintendent of Documents, U.S. Government Printing Office
Internet: bookstore.gpo.gov Phone: toll free (866) 512–1800; DC area (202) 512–1800
Fax: (202) 512–2104 Mail: Stop IDCC, Washington, DC 20402–0001

(II)

# CONTENTS

# WHEN CATASTROPHE STRIKES: RESPONSES TO NATURAL DISASTERS IN INDIAN COUNTRY

## WEDNESDAY, JULY 30, 2014

U.S. SENATE,
COMMITTEE ON INDIAN AFFAIRS,
*Washington, DC.*

The Committee met, pursuant to notice, at 2:47 p.m. in room 628, Dirksen Senate Office Building, Hon. Jon Tester, Chairman of the Committee, presiding.

### OPENING STATEMENT OF HON. JON TESTER, U.S. SENATOR FROM MONTANA

The CHAIRMAN. The Committee will come to order.

Today the Committee is holding an oversight hearing on responses to national disasters in Indian Country, with a particular focus on the relationship between Federal response agencies, specifically FEMA and the tribes that request assistance.

I very much appreciate our witnesses who have traveled to join us today from Alaska, Nevada, New Mexico, Oklahoma, Washington State. Your presence is clear evidence of the importance of the topics that we are going to assess today. I also appreciate our FEMA witness taking time to join us here today.

Past hearings, including the one this Committee held on natural disasters three years ago, laid out the landscape of disaster response needs in Indian Country. In response to those needs, I offered an amendment to the Stafford Act which authorized tribes to request a disasters declaration directly from the President.

Before the amendment, tribes had to work through States to request a disaster declaration. It was slow, uncertain, and altogether an unacceptable solution for some tribes. In this hearing, we want to explore what has happened since the Stafford Act amendment. The ability to make direct requests for disaster declaration is all well and good, but we need to ensure that authority is translating into appropriate and timely Federal assistance. Are tribes getting more response and assistance now than they were before the amendment or are the implementation processes the same?

I want to thank Senator Begich for his work in conducting oversight of FEMA. I am proud that our two staffs have worked together to hold the agency accountable for their work in Indian Country. We appreciate that. We jointly wrote to FEMA Administrator Craig Fugate back in March, urging him to make outreach and consultation with tribes a priority. Senator Begich has been able to question the Administrator on multiple occasions, keeping the focus on development of guidance for tribal disaster declarations. I am interested in hearing today what the witnesses have to say about these topics and other aspects of this important issue that they would like to discuss.

Senator Barrasso, do you have an opening statement?

## STATEMENT OF HON. JOHN BARRASSO, U.S. SENATOR FROM WYOMING

Senator BARRASSO. Yes, thank you, Mr. Chairman, for holding this important hearing. A natural disaster can instantly destroy the infrastructure and resources needed for tribal economies and essential services. It is critical that tribes have the tools they need to mitigate and respond to the damage caused by a natural disaster. These disasters, however, can destroy more than roads, buildings and forests. The disasters can take away precious lives of children, parents and other loved ones.

It is critically important, Mr. Chairman, that Federal, State and tribal responders coordinate effectively to prevent as well as to address natural disasters. With this in mind, I look forward to the hearing and hearing from our witnesses and welcome them here today.

Thank you, Mr. Chairman.

The CHAIRMAN. Before we get to Ms. Zimmerman, does any other member have a statement? Senator Udall.

## STATEMENT OF HON. TOM UDALL, U.S. SENATOR FROM NEW MEXICO

Senator UDALL. Thank you, Chairman Tester. Thank you for holding this important oversight hearing on the impact of catastrophic disasters on Indian Country.

Tribes in New Mexico are no strangers to these disasters, to drought, fire and flooding. It is a vicious cycle and it hits Indian Country especially hard. The historic drought threatens our Native American farmers' livelihood and their way of life. Their forests are ravaged by forest fires. And when the rain does come, their homes are threatened by floods. We can't always stop the fire or hold back the water, but we must ensure that the Federal Government is there to help, to do all we can in rebuilding and preventing further harm.

When disaster strikes Indian Country, tribal leaders need direct government to government communications and resources to help their people. I don't think anyone knows that better than the governor of the Pueblo of Santa Clara, Michael Chavarria. And I am very pleased to introduce him today. Governor Chavarria has served his pueblo for many years not only as governor but also as forestry director, where he was the emergency response coordinator during the Las Conchas fire, at the time the largest wildfire in New Mexico history. He also oversaw the response for the subsequent flooding, flooding that destroyed all the water control structures in Santa Clara Canyon.

He is an outstanding advocate, as the Pueblo faces continued risk of catastrophic flooding. He is also an important voice and one we should listen to carefully in the broader discussion of the effects of climate change, one of the root causes of the disasters that his people have faced with such courage and resilience.

Last September, most New Mexico tribes were impacted by heavy rains and were sub-grantees to the State of New Mexico in the FEMA disaster declaration. The Santa Clara Pueblo was the only Pueblo to meet the criteria for direct assistance and has received two tribally declared declarations. The impacts to Santa Clara are ominous and the flood path goes right towards their traditional village.

But they are not alone. The Pueblo of Cochiti is also working to prevent flooding into its village and to rebuild a critical bridge destroyed in flooding from the Las Conchas fire. The Cochiti, Santo Domingo and Santa Clara Pueblo are actively seeking assistance for post-fire and flooding efforts. Just this month, flooding has hit many pueblos, including Zuni, Ohkay Owingeh, Pojoaque, Santo Domingo, Cochiti, Santa Clara and Jemez. All have reported damage to tribal infrastructure or roads.

Chairman Tester, these needs are crucial. We have to be better and faster to help Indian Country in the wake of disaster. Their ageing infrastructure leaves tribes more at risk to horrific fire and flooding and the lack of resources leaves them ill-prepared to respond. Despite their determination and their best efforts, I hope this hearing will help us to better understand the true impact of these disasters and to deal with them more effectively.

I welcome Governor Chavarria, and I have another commitment and hope to be back for his testimony. Thank you, Chairman Tester, very much.

The CHAIRMAN. Thank you, Senator Udall, very much.

Senator Cantwell?

## STATEMENT OF HON. MARIA CANTWELL, U.S. SENATOR FROM WASHINGTON

Senator CANTWELL. Thank you, Mr. Chairman. I too want to thank you for holding this important hearing and want to welcome one of the witnesses who is going to be on the next panel, Ronda Metcalf. She is currently the Secretary of the Sauk-Suiattle Tribe and is here on behalf of the tribe and the Chairwoman, Norma A. Joseph, who couldn't be with us here today. She is going to talk about her FEMA experiences.

I can think of no better way to honor the relationship of government to government relations than to have that relationship work in a natural disaster, to have an unplanned crisis and then to have the leadership response, you need governments to communicate to other governments.

On March 22nd of this year, State Route 530 had a landslide that occurred and killed 43 people and cut off access to one of our most traveled roads in the Northwest. It became a deadly landslide in our Country. So during this ongoing recovery process, Ms. Metcalf and tribal leaders did their best to do everything they could, even though they were also cut off from medical service and the main route, and meant people going what would have normally have been a half hour route to hospitals or various services to go more than an hour and a half, two hours around and cause much complication.

So I recently visited, Mr. Chairman, with the tribal council at their headquarters to hear about many of the issues that happened in the aftermath of that mudslide. I heard about their experiences with FEMA, and she is going to elaborate on that today.

But I believe that it is a powerful and instructive story to remind us that we need to make sure that when Indian Country makes declarations, just as a governor makes declarations, that those declarations are acted on quickly. That secondly, we have immediate response teams that work well and coordinate with Indian Country, that there are FEMA people on the ground who really do understand the role and responsibility and coordination with Indian Country. And that we understand all of their investments that were made in helping in a time of need and emergency.

It is almost heartbreaking, Mr. Chairman, to see how many people showed up at a gymnasium just three days after the crisis and to see who immediately stood up with resources and money. Three tribes basically came and donated almost $700,000 to the effort from around the community. This tribe, right in the midst of the community, got none of those resources. Yet they put people on overtime pay, they kept their gas station open, they ferried people around for medical services, they did everything a partner could do in that crisis, and yet didn't get any of the support from the entities that needed to help support them, because they too were impacted by the crisis.

So I hope it is all instructive. I hope it was just a miscommunication and that it is not happening anywhere else. But clearly it points out that we just need to flatten these issues moving forward. And certainly as my colleague from New Mexico said, I think it gives us something to think about too, from a communication perspective, the fact that this area was cut off literally from all communication because of where the slide happened. So the town of Darrington and this tribe basically cut off from all the recovery points to this fact that a lot of these areas are remote. So what do we do about emergency communications? Maybe this is something our Committee needs to look at in the future, how do we make sure that these areas have good emergency communication systems, so that they can be utilized, whether it is a flood or tornado or what have you, so we are not out there just basically without the resources that are needed once the disaster strikes.

I thank you for having this hearing, and will look forward to Ms. Metcalf's testimony.

The CHAIRMAN. Thank you for your comments, Senator Cantwell. Senator Begich?

### STATEMENT OF HON. MARK BEGICH, U.S. SENATOR FROM ALASKA

Senator BEGICH. Thank you, Mr. Chairman. Thank you for holding this hearing. It is an important topic. I will try to keep my comments brief. But I also want to give a warm welcome to an Alaska witness who will be on the second panel, Ms. Mary David, visiting all the way from Nome, Alaska. We look forward to hearing her testimony.

In recognizing the challenges of tribal communities as they prepare, respond to and recover from various disasters requires collaboration and cooperation. I have been lucky to work on critical emergency management issues that cut across various Committee assignments and believe that this lends itself well to accomplishing a key goal here in the Senate. As chair of the Homeland Security Subcommittee with jurisdiction over FEMA, I have been working to highlight the need for tribal engagement outreach and resources throughout the agencies. Senator Tester, I want to thank you for the letter we wrote, the response we got, because we both sit on that committee also. It has unique opportunities on that committee and this Committee to push the issue forward.

The new authorities granted to tribes through the Sandy Recovery Improvement Act allow for major disaster declarations to be made directly to the President without having to go through governors. This move puts tribes on par with States and illustrates the sovereignty that government-to-government relationship that has been so critical to making progress and building a strong relationship. But there is work to be done to fully accomplish this.

On his first trip to Alaska. FEMA Administrator Fugate heard a lot, I want to underline that, a lot, about this, when we met with Alaska Native leaders. I believe it is critically important for FEMA leadership to practice what they preach when it comes to meaningful outreach and consultation. Each tribe and village is different, and the threats and hazards they face are equally so. There are real challenges facing our tribes. Coastal erosion is wiping out entire communities in western Alaska. Flooding inundates rural communities along the Yukon and Kuskokwim Rivers in Alaska. Many villages can see real seismic damage or tsunami threat following another catastrophic earthquake.

Mr. Chairman, I think you would agree that FEMA's outreach over the years has been somewhat lacking. I feel tribal affairs structure within the agency does not adequately reflect the critical role that tribal governments and organizations plan in the emergency management community. I am encouraged by the hiring of Milo Booth, Alaska Native Tribal Member, of the Metlakatla Indian Community, to lead tribal affairs in FEMA. I worry, however, that by housing tribal affairs within external affairs or intergovernmental affairs the real impact of regulatory or statutory changes cannot be adequately addressed.

Outreach and meaningful consultation should be done in a way that fosters a partnership, not a one-way push of information or not just checking the box. As you know, Mr. Chairman, the committee that I chair over in Homeland Security will continue to hold FEMA's feet to the fire. We do oversight over there on a regular basis and I appreciate this effort here that you are doing, because it really emphasizes this unique opportunity to allow tribes to exercise their rights as sovereign entities, working with FEMA in the midst of a disaster or recovery from a disaster.

And I would underline, as Senator Udall mentioned, mitigation, as we struggle with the challenges of climate change, what do we do in the future to push back and make sure we have the right kind of mitigation situation.

Thank you, Mr. Chairman.

The CHAIRMAN. Thank you, Senator Begich. I want to welcome Ms. Elizabeth Zimmerman, who is the Deputy Associate Administrator for the Office of Response and Recovery at FEMA. I would just remind you, you have five minutes for your verbal comments. Know that your entire written testimony will be a part of the record. There will be a few questions afterwards. You may proceed, Elizabeth. Thank you.

### STATEMENT OF ELIZABETH ZIMMERMAN, DEPUTY ASSOCIATE ADMINISTRATOR, OFFICE OF RESPONSE AND RECOVERY, FEDERAL EMERGENCY MANAGEMENT AGENCY, U.S. DEPARTMENT OF HOMELAND SECURITY

Ms. ZIMMERMAN. Thank you and good afternoon, Chairman Tester and members of the Committee. I am Elizabeth Zimmerman, I am the Deputy Associate Administrator for the Office of Response and Recovery at FEMA. I am here today with a great opportunity to share FEMA's partnership with our federally-recognized tribal governments and how we have been implementing the new authorities that we received as a part of the Sandy Recovery Improvement Act of 2013, or SRIA, as we call it. I thank the Committee for the many authorities that were included in SRIA in order to improve our programs overall, particularly the provision that allows federally recognized tribes the choice to come in directly to the Federal Government for a request for either an emergency or major disaster declaration independently of the States. I want to emphasize that it is their choice and we appreciate that.

I would also like to thank Senator Tester for your leadership in this area as well as Senator Begich for the great work that we have been able to do and accomplish together. It is much appreciated.

The engagement with the tribal governments is a top priority for Administrator Fugate and all the leadership at FEMA. That is why he has advocated for the change, for the Stafford Act, pretty much since he got here five years ago, to make sure that we reflect the tribal sovereignty and the self-determination for the tribes. I have been overseeing the implementation of the authority and our continued partnership with tribal governments on response and recovery efforts.

When we started it, as soon as SRIA passed, we were able to implement three phases for the disaster declarations. The first thing we were able to do is use the current regulations that we have while we were out doing consultation and putting together draft pilot guidance, which is out right now for public comment. The next step after that will be regulations.

So immediately after the Act was enacted, we put the new authority out there, available for tribal governments to use the existing declaration's regulations, which provided us the ability to afford them the opportunity to come in directly to the President for the disaster declaration request. As soon as possible, providing an avenue to learn from these declarations, in order to solidify the government to government relationship that we have. To date seven tribal governments have requested eight disaster declarations. The President has declared six major disaster declarations for tribes.

FEMA has been consulting with the tribal governments on tribal declarations implementation. We wanted to be thoughtful and deliberate to develop the procedures that would reflect the unique circumstances of those tribal governments.

Since FEMA initiated the tribal consultation on the first draft of the declaration's pilot guidance, we have undertaken one of the largest engagement efforts in this agency's history, the largest tribal consultation effort by far. To date we have held 55 in-person meetings to discuss the guidance with over 500 tribal participants representing 220 tribes. For example, in FEMA's Region 10, which is situated in the State of Washington, leadership has held seven listening sessions, across Alaska, from St. Paul Island to the Bering Sea, to Barrow and the Arctic Slope.

Working with tribal organizations we have held five meetings across California, the State with the second highest number of federally-recognized tribes. Over 30 tribes have participated in new sessions.

From Montana to the Midwest, Florida, Maine, FEMA leadership across the Country have been out there to talk with tribes face to face about the tribal guidance, discuss the Stafford Act and to make available resources, listening to the feedback and to enhance our government to government relationship.

After this consultation, we will revise the draft guidance based on the input we have received. The revised draft will then be published in the Federal Register, for which we will hold another round of tribal consultation.

The agency is also collaborating with the tribes to develop a tribal consultation policy separate from the declarations policy in order to provide instruction and guidance for FEMA employees on how to engage in tribal governments on FEMA actions that have tribal implications. Through grants, training, outreach and technical assistance, we are also helping tribes prepare for and protect against, respond to, recover from and mitigate against disasters. To ensure that tribes are informed about these opportunities for assistance, as was mentioned, we have hired Milo Booth, an Alaska Native, who is sitting here as our National Tribal Affairs Advisor.

In conclusion, I would like to say that FEMA is one part of emergency management. Our tribal nations are another key critical component of an emergency management team. And we are committed to consulting, coordinating and engaging with federally-recognized tribal governments in the development and implementation of all of our policies and programs that impact them.

We look forward to continuing our collaboration with tribes and this Committee to ensure that we are fully supportive and engage with the tribal nations. Thank you and I look forward to any questions.

[The prepared statement of Ms. Zimmerman follows:]

PREPARED STATEMENT OF ELIZABETH ZIMMERMAN, DEPUTY ASSOCIATE ADMINISTRATOR, OFFICE OF RESPONSE AND RECOVERY, FEDERAL EMERGENCY MANAGEMENT AGENCY, U.S. DEPARTMENT OF HOMELAND SECURITY

**Introduction**

Good afternoon, Chairman Tester, Vice Chairman Barrasso and members of the Committee. I am Elizabeth Zimmerman, Deputy Associate Administrator of the Office of Response and Recovery (ORR) of the Department of Homeland Security's (DHS) Federal Emergency Management Agency (FEMA). Thank you for the opportunity to discuss FEMA's partnerships with federally recognized tribal governments, and how we are implementing new authorities to work directly with tribal governments as part of the "Sandy Recovery Improvement Act of 2013" (SRIA).

I would like to take this opportunity to thank the Committee for the authority established in SRIA, including the provision that allows a federally recognized tribe the choice to request Stafford Act emergency and major disaster declarations independently of states. I would also like to thank Senator Tester for his leadership in this area.

The engagement of tribal governments is a top priority for Administrator Fugate. He advocated for changes in the Stafford Act to reflect tribal self-determination and provide tribal governments the choice to seek federal disaster assistance through a state or directly to FEMA. The passage of SRIA was a major milestone in these efforts, but was just the first step in fully implementing this important authority. FEMA continues consulting with tribal governments on tribal declarations implementation, including the development of the Tribal Declarations Pilot Guidance.

FEMA supports federally recognized tribal governments, and their sovereignty and rights of self-determination as a part of the federal trust responsibility to Tribal Nations. In addition, inclusion of Tribal Nations is an essential component of FEMA's whole community emergency management strategy.

## Foundational Policies and Strategic Context

### Foundational Policies

FEMA has a historical commitment to enhancing government-to-government relations with tribal nations. The first FEMA Tribal Policy was created in 1998 and revised in 2010. FEMA further revised and reissued the policy in late 2013 for an additional three years. This policy forges a commitment to strong and lasting partnerships by outlining the guiding principles of engagement and collaboration between FEMA and federally recognized American Indian and Alaska Native Tribal governments.

FEMA follows guidance outlined in the President's November 5, 2009 Memorandum on Tribal Consultation. This Memorandum reaffirms Executive Order (E.O.) 13175, directing agencies to engage in regular and meaningful consultation and collaboration with tribal officials in the development of Federal policies that have tribal implications, and to strengthen the government-to-government relationship between the United States and Tribal Nations. FEMA is drafting, in coordination and consultation with Tribal Nations, a Tribal Consultation Policy, which will supplement the DHS Tribal Consultation Policy. FEMA received valuable input and comments that are being adjudicated into the final Tribal Consultation Policy, which will be used as a framework for future consultation between FEMA and Tribal Nations.

### Strategic Context

FEMA's whole community approach reinforces the fact that FEMA is only one part of our nation's emergency management team. We must leverage all of our collective team resources in preparing for, protecting against, responding to, recovering from and mitigating against all hazards. Tribal Nations are critical components in our whole community, and our commitment to addressing their needs is evident in our strategic priority to be survivor-centric in mission and program delivery. To further survivor-centric goals, FEMA leadership adopted a "cut the red tape" posture to focus on the needs of survivors and to develop and execute programs and policies with survivors' perspectives in mind.

FEMA recognizes that the consistent participation and partnership of tribal governments is vital in helping FEMA achieve its mission.

## Tribal Declarations Under the Sandy Recovery Improvement Act

On January 29, 2013, President Obama signed into law, the "Disaster Relief Appropriations Act, 2013" (Division A) and SRIA (Division B) respectively of Public Law 113–2, a legislative package authorizing several significant changes to the way FEMA delivers disaster assistance. SRIA is one of the most significant pieces of legislation impacting disaster response and recovery since the Post-Katrina Emergency Management Reform Act of 2006.

Section 1110 of SRIA, "Tribal Requests for a Major Disaster or Emergency Declaration under the Stafford Act" authorized federally recognized tribal governments the option to request a Stafford Act emergency or major disaster declaration independent of the State where their lands are located. This new authority also requires the Federal Government to "consider the unique conditions that affect the general welfare of tribal governments" when developing regulations to implement this new authority. FEMA has developed a phased implementation to ensure we consider the unique needs of tribal governments, which are further outlined below.

*Phased Implementation of Direct Tribal Declarations*

In consultation with our nation's federally recognized tribes, we are working thoughtfully and deliberately to develop procedures that best reflect the unique situation of tribal governments. Therefore, FEMA is implementing direct tribal declarations in three phases: (1) through the use of current regulations; (2) through the development and implementation of pilot guidance; and (3) through notice and comment rulemaking.

*Use of Current Regulations*

Immediately after SRIA's enactment, FEMA used existing declaration regulations and criteria to process declaration requests from tribal governments. Eight disaster requests have been made, with six major disaster declarations issued for five tribes: the Eastern Band of Cherokee Indians, the Navajo Nation, the Standing Rock Sioux Tribe, the Karuk Tribe, and the Santa Clara Pueblo Tribe, which has received two disaster declarations. Through these declarations, Public Assistance and Hazard Mitigation Grant Program funding is being provided directly to the tribes. The damage assessment information regarding these declarations is outlined in Table 1 below in the order of their declaration date.

### TABLE 1: PUBLIC ASSISTANCE PRELIMINARY DAMAGE ASSESSMENT ESTIMATES—TRIBAL DECLARATIONS

| Tribal Government | Declaration Date | Preliminary Damage Assessment Estimate |
|---|---|---|
| Eastern Band of Cherokee Indians (DR–4103) | 3/1/2013 | $3,161,875 |
| Navajo Nation (DR–4104) | 3/5/2013 | $5,223,234 |
| Standing Rock Sioux Tribe (DR–4123) | 6/25/2013 | $1,277,493 |
| Karuk Tribe (DR–4142) | 8/29/2013 | $1,021,557 |
| Santa Clara Pueblo (DR–4147) | 9/27/2013 | $5,393,852 |
| Santa Clara Pueblo (DR–4151) | 10/24/2013 | $1,984,960 |

Through these declarations, FEMA gathered critical information, best practices, and process challenges that have informed the development of the Tribal Declarations Pilot Guidance, which is the second phase of tribal declarations implementation.

*Pilot Guidance Development*

We recognize that FEMA's current declarations regulations were developed to evaluate States' capacity and their need for supplemental disaster assistance. Since these parameters may not be indicative of a Tribal Nation's ability to respond and recover from a disaster, FEMA determined the need to develop procedures and criteria that reflect the capacity and needs of tribal governments. Before entering the rulemaking process to codify the tribal-specific procedures, FEMA will initiate a pilot program to ensure that final regulations sufficiently reflect the unique needs of tribal governments.

Soon after SRIA was signed, FEMA engaged tribal governments on the current procedures to process declarations and whether those procedures should be revised for direct tribal declarations. FEMA used this initial input to develop a first draft of the Tribal Declarations Pilot Guidance.

Tribal participation and input is critical to the development of the Tribal Declarations Pilot Guidance. On April 3, 2014, we initiated tribal consultation on the draft guidance. FEMA sent written correspondence from Administrator Fugate to all 566 federally recognized tribes and issued advisories to national and regional tribal organizations and associations to advise them of the consultation. FEMA Regional and Headquarters leadership also presented at numerous tribal conferences to provide an overview of the declaration process and the draft guidance.

Between April 3 and July 8, 2014, FEMA conducted 45 listening sessions around the country, from Northern Alaska to Montana, Oklahoma to Florida, and to Maine with 445 participants and 189 tribes represented. Through these listening sessions, FEMA gathered input on the draft guidance as well as strengthened relationships with tribal governments. We learned more about the challenges that tribal communities face, the response and recovery capabilities of tribal governments, and their understanding of Stafford Act assistance. FEMA regions have been extremely proactive in meeting consultation requests of Native Alaskan Villages and Indian tribal governments. For instance, FEMA Region X consulted with the Aleut Communities of St. Paul and St. George Islands on St. Paul Island Alaska.

The information gathered in these sessions will be used to revise the draft guidance. This revised draft will be published for public comment and a second round of tribal consultation, continuing our commitment to engage tribal governments in the implementation of tribal declarations.

*Regulations*

As required by SRIA, FEMA will begin development of regulations after the pilot guidance is finalized. This will follow the standard notice and comment rulemaking process.

## Tribal Grants

Tribal governments and their members are an essential part of our nation's emergency management team, and FEMA is committed to supporting our tribal partners in its efforts to build more resilient and better prepared communities. The Tribal Homeland Security Grant Program (THSGP) supports the building, sustainment, and delivery of core capabilities to enable tribes to strengthen their capacity to prepare for, protect against, respond to, recover from, and mitigate potential terrorist attacks and other hazards. Federally recognized tribes that meet the criteria as outlined in the Homeland Security Act of 2002, as amended, are eligible for direct funding. This law prescribes a minimum allocation of .01 percent of the total funds allocated for all grants under Sections 2003 and 2004 of the Homeland Security Act of 2002, as amended. However, FEMA and Department of Homeland Security Headquarters increased that amount to an average of $10 million per year for the past three years. Since the program was initiated in FY 2008, more than 150 tribal applications have been funded with approximately $50 million for capacity and capability building under the THSGP.

Federally recognized tribes are eligible for other pre-disaster grant funding such as Assistance to Firefighters Grants and Hazard Mitigation.

## Tribal Consultation Policy

In recognition of the Federal Government's trust responsibilities and to honor and continue to enhance our partnerships with federally recognized tribes and in accordance with the 2009 Presidential Memorandum and E.O. 13175, FEMA is collaborating with tribes to develop a Tribal Consultation Policy. This policy supplements the DHS Tribal Consultation Policy by providing additional instructions and guidance to FEMA employees on engagement of tribal governments for consultation on FEMA actions with tribal implications. It also ensures FEMA is effectively engaging in regular and meaningful consultation and collaboration with our tribal partners.

The policy is being developed based on discussion, input and consultation with tribes to ensure it addresses their concerns and reflects a government-to-government relationship with Tribal Nations. The consultation period for the proposed Tribal Consultation Policy ended on March 30, 2014. FEMA is currently in a thoughtful review of the input received, and is revising the Policy as appropriate. FEMA will notify tribes when the policy is published, which is planned for later this year. The Tribal Consultation Policy will help govern how FEMA undertakes future consultation with tribes.

## Training, Outreach and Technical Assistance Efforts

FEMA is committed to helping tribes prepare for, protect against, respond to, recover from, and mitigate against disasters through its training, outreach and technical assistance efforts. FEMA's National Tribal Affairs Advisor, Milo Booth, works closely with the FEMA Regional Tribal Liaisons and programs to ensure that tribes are informed about these opportunities for assistance.

*Training*

FEMA's Emergency Management Institute (EMI) offered the first tribal-specific course, titled ''Emergency Management Framework for Tribal Governments'' in January of 2002. This course was developed in collaboration with tribal emergency services and emergency management personnel. In the 12 years since, EMI's Tribal Curriculum has grown to five tribal-specific courses. Continuing from the success of the first tribal course, all of these courses were designed with input from tribal representatives and associations and are intended to help build emergency management capability in tribal communities. To date, more than 3,000 certificates of completion have been issued for courses in the EMI Tribal Curriculum. These courses include ''Emergency Management Framework for Tribal Governments,'' ''Emergency Operations for Tribal Governments,'' ''Mitigation for Tribal Governments,'' ''Continuity of Operations (COOP) for Tribal Governments,'' and ''Emergency Management Overview for Tribal Leaders.'' Between fiscal year (FY) 2011 and 2013, 1,174 students, of which 998 are tribal government employees and 715 are American Indian or Alaska Native members, completed the five tribal-specific courses. In FY 2013, 466 students participated in these courses, which were held in locations across the country, including Arizona, California, Nevada, North Carolina, Oklahoma, and Washington. Additionally, tribal emergency management officials have access to 550 active courses offered through EMI.

*Outreach*

The FEMA National Tribal Affairs Advisor and other FEMA leadership, regularly attend the annual and mid-year meetings hosted by the National Congress of American Indians (NCAI), the United South and Eastern Tribes (USET), the National Tribal Emergency Management Council (NTEMC), Tribal Assistance Coordination Group (TAC–G), and the Tribal Emergency Management Association (iTEMA) as well as other regional and national tribal organizations and associations. These meetings provide FEMA the opportunity to conduct outreach and establish a stronger working relationship with these organizations. FEMA's Office of External Affairs also facilitates information sharing across the Agency before, during and after disasters that impact tribal communities.

In 2011, FEMA announced an initiative through FEMA's Ready Campaign called *"Ready Indian Country." Ready Indian Country* is an initiative designed to promote preparedness within tribal communities through education and outreach in an effort to save lives and prevent property losses. The program, developed with the support of NCAI, uses public outreach and the support of tribal elders to encourage members of Tribal Nations to take the basic steps necessary to prepare themselves for potential emergencies. *Ready Indian Country* provides a foundation for tribal communities to enhance citizen preparedness while serving as a resource for the development and implementation of community pre-disaster policies and procedures.

*Ready Indian Country*'s resources include existing Ready Campaign messaging and build on existing capacity with specific tools customized for Indian Country. These include brochures, posters and billboards customized by geographic region to reflect diverse local conditions and American Indian and Alaska Native cultures; radio Public Service Announcements (PSAs) in 60, 30 and 15 second formats; and Tribal Leader Resources to help guide community emergency planning efforts. *Ready Indian Country* resources can be found at *http://www.ready.gov/IndianCountry*. This is one step in the ongoing actions on the part of FEMA and the Ready Campaign to nurture this partnership to help tribes and Native American communities build sustainable and resilient tribal neighborhoods.

*Technical Assistance*

The FEMA Regional Tribal Liaisons and the FEMA National Tribal Affairs Advisor serve as tribes' initial entry into FEMA to facilitate discussions between tribes and subject matter experts, to share information, or address questions or challenges. In addition to its dedicated liaisons and Advisor, FEMA as a whole is dedicated to ensuring we consult and effectively collaborate with tribal governments, whether during a disaster, the development of policy, or program implementation.

Additionally, in coordination with FEMA Regional Tribal Liaisons, the Technical Assistance (TA) Program provides specialized emergency management planning assistance to tribes across the nation. This helps tribes to develop operational plans and to be prepared for disasters or emergencies. Specifically, the TA program works with tribes to build capacity, educate their leaders in foundational emergency management concepts, and enhance relationships among emergency managers and planners across the state, local, tribal and federal levels of government.

Since 2011, FEMA has hosted 13 working sessions and workshops to engage tribes. When the Bureau of Indian Affairs stood up their Division of Emergency Management in 2013, FEMA increased its partnership effort with them to deliver tribal TA to the nation's federally recognized tribes, ensuring even stronger federal coordination in support of tribal governments.

## Additional Tribal Efforts

*Tribal Integration Group*

FEMA established an internal Tribal Integration Group (TIG) this year, which serves as an internal coordinating body for tribal-related engagement and consultation across FEMA programs. The TIG, co-led by FEMA Senior Executives—the Deputy Director of the Office of External Affairs and the Director of the DHS Center for Faith-based & Neighborhood Partnerships—is working to ensure that the Agency meets requirements to consult and collaborate with and consider tribal governments needs in the Agency's program and policy development.

In addition, the TIG strengthens efforts to engage tribal governments in FEMA's processes, procedures and outreach. The TIG is also in the process of assessing long-term resource and organizational strategies to build a stronger relationship with tribal nations throughout the Agency.

The TIG not only serves as an internal coordinating body for tribal-related engagement and issues across FEMA programs and the Agency as a whole; it is also a tool for FEMA to discuss and consider high-level tribal issues for recommended action.

**Conclusion**

FEMA is committed to consulting, coordinating, and engaging with federally recognized tribal governments in the development and implementation of policy and programs.

We are grateful to Congress for these new authorities and are actively working with the sovereign tribes as they prepare for, protect against, respond to, recover from, and mitigate against the hazards they may face.

We look forward to our continued collaboration to further support tribal governments as they build their emergency management capabilities. Thank you.

The CHAIRMAN. Thank you, Ms. Zimmerman, for your testimony.

I will start. I think FEMA has been working on developing connections with tribal governments and trying to get the right information to the right people. That being said, we hear from folks in Indian Country regularly that they don't know who to get hold of or how to get in touch with the folks who are going to help them when they do have a disaster.

Could you talk about FEMA's efforts to increase information sharing and points of contact for tribal communities?

Ms. ZIMMERMAN. Sure, I would be happy to. When it comes to coordination, as you know, FEMA has 10 regions across the United States. Our regional administrators all have a tribal liaison officer within their offices. They are a conduit to the rest of the FEMA staff, over 5,000 of us that exist across the Country. So the tribal liaisons, the regional administrators and their staff are reaching out to the tribes in order to make them aware of the tribal guidance, going out and sitting down with them to get their comments, that is the conduit. We are happy to provide to you the names of those, the tribal liaison officers. We can get that to you, as well as the regional administrators.

The CHAIRMAN. So the tribal liaison, just for example, in Montana, would be located where?

Ms. ZIMMERMAN. That is in our Region 8, which is in Denver, Colorado.

The CHAIRMAN. So are they actually going to the tribes? How many States do they have? How many States does that tribal liaison cover?

Ms. ZIMMERMAN. I believe Region 8 has six States.

The CHAIRMAN. And it would be all of——

Ms. ZIMMERMAN. It is Colorado, Utah, Montana, North and South Dakota and Wyoming.

The CHAIRMAN. So you have a fair number of Indian folks who live in those six States.

Ms. ZIMMERMAN. Yes.

The CHAIRMAN. Are they going to the tribes? Are they going actually into—I will pick a tribe—Crow?

Ms. ZIMMERMAN. What they have done is they have both gone out to meet with tribes as well as they have convened meetings. Additionally, we have provided invitational travel for the tribal members to come to meetings to bring more together at once place.

The CHAIRMAN. Okay. You guys do good work. I think that the outreach is always a continuing challenge, especially with this program, which is fairly new. Letting those folk know when they have a flood event or a fire event or whatever the event might be who to get hold of is critically important.

Up-front costs for FEMA, if the tribes are dealing directly with you instead of the State, the up-front costs, in the case of many of the poorer tribes, is a real problem. Whereas if they go through the State, the State oftentimes picks that up, they have a few more resources than the tribes do. Is there anything FEMA can do about those up-front costs, to help reduce them where the tribe is directly contracting?

Ms. ZIMMERMAN. Are you referring to the cost share?

The CHAIRMAN. Yes.

Ms. ZIMMERMAN. Yes, because under the Stafford Act, the Federal Government pays no less than 75 percent. So the 25 percent, is borne by the grantee or sub-grantees. So that is something that we are looking at. That has been raised among the over 800 comments that we have already received on the draft tribal guidance. We look for folks to give input into that and suggestions as to how they would address that and how they would like to see that come out.

So it is something that we are very well aware of.

The CHAIRMAN. So you have started that comment period already?

Ms. ZIMMERMAN. Yes. The comment period started on April 3rd and we put it out there and we have just extended it, it was due to expire today.

The CHAIRMAN. Can you give me an idea of how many contacts you have gotten from tribes on this issue?

Ms. ZIMMERMAN. We have had over 800 comments so far.

The CHAIRMAN. On this issue?

Ms. ZIMMERMAN. On the declarations tribal guidance.

The CHAIRMAN. Okay. I think Senator Begich talked about this in his opening statement, the placement of the tribal all-hazards emergency response office in FEMA's external affairs, apart from the Office of Response and Recovery. What is the best place for this office? Is it really in External Affairs?

Ms. ZIMMERMAN. Since I am the Deputy for the Office of Response and Recovery, I have direct access to Milo and he has direct access to me, as well as everyone else in FEMA leadership. So to us, it is fine, because they have the access that they need and can get the information and we share information very regularly.

The CHAIRMAN. All right. Senator Murkowski?

## STATEMENT OF HON. LISA MURKOWSKI, U.S. SENATOR FROM ALASKA

Senator MURKOWSKI. Mr. Chairman, I appreciate your being here this afternoon.

I want to talk a little bit about the Galena experience in interior Alaska, but I want you to keep in mind that that is just one episode of a disaster in rural Alaska that we have so many more. But Galena is going to be my focal point today. We see so much in terms of the planning that I think FEMA puts in place for the buildup into the hurricane season, for instance, into the Gulf. We have different seasons around the lower 48, hurricanes, tornadoes, well, in Alaska, we have ice jam season. It comes every spring. Sometimes it is a season that is without event and other times it is a season that really writes the history book.

But it seems like the disaster managers, we write the book in terms of how to deal with these disasters every year, which is very, very frustrating. It seems like all the decisions that need to be made need to be coordinated with headquarters all the way back in places like Washington, D.C.

Galena is a specific example. There are two ways to get things into Galena, by barge, and there are a couple barges a season, or fly them in. So there is no rocket science here, there is no road to Home Depot. It is a very short time period. The Inspector General, when we asked him to look at the disaster situation in Galena, he comes back and he says, he criticized FEMA for not leaning forward, flying the materials in rather than going through this check the box exercise.

I have asked for this review, we got it back from the IG, but there were lessons from Galena, as one example. But more emblematic of the problem that we have all over Alaska when it comes to remoteness, inability to access, by traditional methods, which are roads. How have we learned from that going forward?

Now, we had an opportunity last week in the Appropriations Committee to visit with Administrator Fugate to address the IG's findings with respect to the deficiencies with tribal collaboration during that event. He suggests that we now have this new tribal consultation policy. I look at that and say, well, okay. We have FEMA that views tribes as partners rather than grantees or perhaps sub-grantees. If that is what is necessary, maybe we need to look at things that way.

But we have had a tribal policy in place in FEMA since 1989. So how are we at this point where again it seems like we are reinventing with every disaster that comes? How is it that FEMA works so much better, seemingly, with the States, than they do with the tribes? What have we learned from Galena going forward? Because as sure as winter is going to come, spring is going to follow and we are going to have flooding in interior Alaska.

Ms. ZIMMERMAN. Yes, it is a continuous thing and I can appreciate it. I was up there in Galena this last year.

Senator MURKOWSKI. I thank you for that.

Ms. ZIMMERMAN. There were disasters in 2010, when you have to fly from place to place, like you said, you don't drive, and there is not a Home Depot around the corner. I can appreciate that, and it is something that we continue to try to be better at.

Senator MURKOWSKI. But have we changed things in order to be better at, or are we just hoping that next time we get a little luckier?

Ms. ZIMMERMAN. No, we have been changing things as far as being able to document what we have done and try to learn from our lessons. It is something that we haven't been the best at in the past, really learning from our lessons. But really taking an honest look at ourselves, after that disaster, and what can we do better, and put something in place in order to implement it so we are ready to go.

For the last five years, we have been trying to lean forward much more by having things ready when we see something coming. We know that earthquakes can happen at any moment, like they do in Alaska, some of those very large earthquakes that happened and the tsunamis that can follow and impact other people very quickly.

Senator MURKOWSKI. One of the observations that we have seen now is that we are not using sufficient numbers of folks that are on the ground. The Native people who live in the villages, what we get instead are these groups of well-meaning folk who are coming up from the outside. But I have always questioned whether or not we rely enough on those who are on the ground, who understand the conditions, who know that you can't do anything beyond September 15th because it is getting cold and freeze-up is coming, as opposed to somebody here in Washington, D.C. that looks at the calendar and says, we still have four months left in the year, this is not a problem.

So what are we doing to increase the number of Native people in the reservist cadres? Can FEMA be doing more in this regard? I think you need to have people on the ground that are giving you that practical advice, rather than having this top-heavy approach.

Ms. ZIMMERMAN. Having people in the field trained in emergency management and being able to communicate back to us through our regional administrator who is on the ground or the folks in the Alaska area office to be coordinating with them ahead of time; this the best thing that you can do so that we are prepared and that we know how we are going to communicate in disasters so as they are working with them, to get us information. That is the focal point, not back here in Washington, D.C., but that regional administrator, that regional office that we have.

Senator MURKOWSKI. But that regional office is still thousands of miles away.

Ms. ZIMMERMAN. Right.

Senator MURKOWSKI. So how we can truly use the local people, not somebody who works in Seattle or even Fairbanks, but somebody who lives in Galena, that is where I would like to see us go. Let's rely on that local knowledge.

Thank you, Mr. Chairman.

The CHAIRMAN. Senator Cantwell?

Senator CANTWELL. Thank you, Mr. Chairman. I share my colleagues' thoughts and frustrations, having actually been to Galena, but also seeing this in the Northwest.

So I have a few questions for you. She is bringing up an interesting point. When I think about the mayor of Darrington, the town of just a few thousand people, he had no capacity, really, either, he and the police chief and everyone else. So somebody from the Forest Service came over and became basically his deputy.

So what she is saying is there are tribal people who could become part of the response team, workforce, everything. They are there, and they know the region. So I would encourage you to look at that.

Does FEMA have protocols for dealing with Indian Country, protocols that say, this is how you work with Indian Country on a declaration, this is how you work with them on government to government assistance, this is how you work with them on individual assistance? Do you think that is clear within FEMA?

Ms. ZIMMERMAN. We have cultural sensitivity training that we give to people in disasters. Back when I was with a State, working in emergency management, and we were working very closely with our tribal partners, and FEMA provided that type of expertise so that people do know. And we do provide training to our disaster reservists, so that they can understand the cultural uniqueness of our tribal partners.

I have to say that the current consultation process that we are undergoing for this declaration guidance is bringing more and more of that to light to us as to how to work and communicate better. So I see going forward as we are drafting this guidance that there will be more protocols established as we develop our consultation policy for FEMA. That policy will be due out this fall.

Senator CANTWELL. I heard about all the listening sessions. I think that is good in general, but it is not about the listening sessions, it is about how do you respond in an emergency.

So on a declaration, once a governor makes a declaration, how often does it usually take an administration to respond to that?

Ms. ZIMMERMAN. Depending on the disaster declaration, some of these things that are immediate, they have been turned around in 90 minutes. Now, that is not the usual, but that is when we really need to get some direct Federal assistance. Typically they are turned around within a matter of days to a week.

Senator CANTWELL. So it took 19 days for the Sauk-Suiattle to get an emergency declaration. Do you have any idea why?

Ms. ZIMMERMAN. I believe that is because we didn't get it directly from the State.

Senator CANTWELL. Why would you have to get it from the State, if they are their own entity and they sent it?

Ms. ZIMMERMAN. Because a declaration request came in through the State of Washington.

Senator CANTWELL. Are we saying that that is what the norm is? Are we saying that every tribe has to go through their State?

Ms. ZIMMERMAN. No, they have a choice.

Senator CANTWELL. Why can't they just make their own declaration?

Ms. ZIMMERMAN. They can if they submit it directly to FEMA.

Senator CANTWELL. I think this is where I would establish a protocol. I would establish a really clear protocol about how that works and make sure everybody knows that and understands it. It is hard, because the same tribe isn't always going to be hit by assistance and come back to FEMA. But if everybody at FEMA knows, that we really do want an immediate response to time for tribes as well, we want to do as well as we do with governors, we want to do, if they have asked for assistance and we want to honor that as quickly as possible.

And then as it relates to, I just want to clarify this point. You can have government, just as the city of Darrington could apply to FEMA and have government assistance, so could a tribe. So the reimbursements or extraordinary expenses related to the natural disaster?

Ms. ZIMMERMAN. So yes, the city of Darrington is a sub-grantee to the State and they can come in and apply.

Senator CANTWELL. And the tribe could do it as well?

Ms. ZIMMERMAN. Yes.

Senator CANTWELL. Without going through the State?

Ms. ZIMMERMAN. Well, the city of Darrington cannot go and—the disaster declaration is made. Once that is made, if it is through the States, then it goes through the State. But if tribes come in directly, like the Santa Clara Pueblo, then it goes directly from FEMA to the tribe.

Senator CANTWELL. Okay. I think this is where we need clarity. A tribe can ask, just like a government entity and can receive assistance and it should do so expeditiously. And I again just thank you, Mr. Chairman, and wholeheartedly agree, you know, we are also dealing with the fires in the Northwest now. And yes, there are some tribal impacts, too. Everybody will tell you, just as in Oso and Darrington, just as in Galena, the local community is so devastated, they want to help. It is the best thing they can do, is to get in there and help.

And FEMA did a great job in Darrington and Oso in letting the locals run the show, even when FEMA came in. It did so much, so much pride, even the President of the United States pointed that out when he came there, the local community stepped up. So I just hope that FEMA will look at ways to let the local tribal communities step up even more. Thank you.

The CHAIRMAN. Senator Udall?

Senator UDALL. I am going to pass, thank you, Mr. Chairman.

The CHAIRMAN. Senator Heitkamp?

## STATEMENT OF HON. HEIDI HEITKAMP, U.S. SENATOR FROM NORTH DAKOTA

Senator HEITKAMP. Thank you, Mr. Chairman.

Obviously North Dakota is no stranger to disaster. We have had two major floods, both affecting the Mandan, Hidatsa and Arikira Nation, Standing Rock Sioux Nation and the continuing slow drip of the rising lake in Devil's Lake, which is affecting Spirit Lake. So a lot of these issues continue to provide unique challenges to Indian people and to my tribes in North Dakota.

It is hard for those of us who have seen kind of the State side of this and the local, whether it is community development block grants, whether it is SBA loans, whether it is those kinds of tools that FEMA routinely uses to help in recovery. It is heartbreaking to see those same tools not being particularly effective in Indian Country.

So where we talk about having the declaration done, respectful government to government relationship, making sure that the FEMA workers who are on the ground to do the evaluation have cultural sensitivity as well as a familiarity with the workers. I want to examine just for a minute the kinds of typical things that FEMA does in response, let's say, to a flood, and whether in your experience you have seen that those tools are not particularly adaptive or capable of being adapted to Indian Country.

Ms. ZIMMERMAN. I believe the tools and the way we respond can be very adaptive. As you know, when a disaster happens it is at

18

the most local level on that tribal government's community. So as
they are responding and as they need assistance and come up
through FEMA, through our regions, to be able to get that extra
assistance, they make that call to the FEMA region. That is why
I encourage and ask all of you to assist us to make sure to get the
word out so that each one of the tribal leaders understand who the
regional administrator is that they can work with to be out there.
So needs are identified, such as if you need assistance through a
mission assignment to the Corps of Engineers—A lot of flood fighting happens up in North Dakota area—where the tribes are impacted. To be able to get that type of assistance, they would come
in through a regional administrator to ask for that and to be able
to get that out there.

Senator HEITKAMP. I would like you to focus not just on a flood
fight, or on the immediacy of dealing with the emergency, but recovery.

Ms. ZIMMERMAN. When it comes to recovery, the same types of
assets are programs. Having the Sandy Recovery Improvement Act
and being able to deal government to government has been the
first key to that. But then to take a look at our programs and how
we administer them—whether it is public assistance for the infrastructure rebuilding or individual assistance program for those individuals impacted by the disaster—and how we can now take and
learn from our consultation process what the impacts of our programs are and how we can work better with the tribal nations. I
think that is key and that is something that we are learning and
getting comments through the consultation.

Senator HEITKAMP. Yes, and maybe just to prove my point, how
many SBA loans do you think have been done in Indian Country
in response to a declaration or disaster relief?

Ms. ZIMMERMAN. I have no idea.

Senator HEITKAMP. You wouldn't. What is the total dollar
amount that has been allocated back to individual families who
have suffered damages either in the basement and may not have
flood insurance?

Ms. ZIMMERMAN. Right now——

Senator HEITKAMP. You see my point, I think. You see my point,
which is that a lot of what is mitigation for families, I am not talking about government relief, government to government relief, but
I am talking about the kinds of tools that come to help families and
homeowners recover. They are not tools that are particularly, I
don't think, effective in Indian Country. I think it is important to
understand those barriers, whether they are home ownership or
whether they are—whatever it is that creates a unique situation in
terms of dealing individually with Indian people and recovery.

Just as an example, since I have been there, Turtle Mountain
lost a roof on a school as a result of a high wind. There wasn't
enough money, they turned to the State, the State wasn't particularly responsive. They turned to us and hopefully we got things
taken care of.

There should be a program in place, or a government to government relationship that you have established with the Turtle Mountain Band of Chippewa so that they have the understanding when

this happens to their community, these are the kinds of assistance that can help.

I think one of the urging in your consultation and in your discussion is to run through those programs that typically provide support in the event of a flood or in the event of an emergency and see how those have been deployed or if they have ever been deployed in Indian Country on tribal trust land. And then think broadly about how can we change the outcome so that someone in Bismarck, North Dakota, who is within the jurisdiction of a disaster plan is, there is parity between that and Indian people living in Indian Country.

The CHAIRMAN. Senator Begich?

Senator BEGICH. Thank you, Mr. Chairman.

Let me, if I can, and I might have missed something, because I was out on a call. So let me ask a couple of questions. I know when the Galena incident occurred in Alaska, the Tanana Chiefs and others were able to provide technical assistance to the tribe and community there.

Can you tell me, is FEMA at this point now fully staffed and organized to really move forward on a sustainable relationship with tribes, not only in Alaska but throughout the Country? Can you give me a sense of where you are? I know we had some discussion and some work that I know Senator Tester did and I did regarding allocation of resources and I know you moved some money around within that organization, I think around close to $800,000, which is good. But are you staffed up enough and do you think you have a capacity now to be sustainable in building these relationships so the technical assistance can also come from, obviously, your organization?

Ms. ZIMMERMAN. Right. Yes, as I was mentioning, we have the 10 regional tribal liaisons, each one in our regions. But that is really just the conduit into getting —

Senator BEGICH. All staffed?

Ms. ZIMMERMAN. Yes. And we have Milo Booth back here, that has just started with FEMA headquarters. He has some folks working with him. But really, the key is that all 5,000 FEMA employees have the ability to provide technical assistance to tribal governments, just like we do anybody else in emergency management. Everyone is committed to this effort for the programs, because they are the subject matter experts.

Senator BEGICH. Can you tell me, help me understand the outreach capacity? In other words, having tribes understand what the role is and responsibility or obligations they might have, what is the steps that you will be doing? I know that was one of the concerns we had, that you had such a small budget at one point that you can't get out to the communities. Where are you on this now with the money that has been allocated, or you have reallocated, I should say? Tell me where you are.

Ms. ZIMMERMAN. To date, we have held 54 listening sessions. We have had over 220 tribes —

Senator BEGICH. Can I pause you for a second? I don't meant to interrupt you, but the listening sessions are to gather what their concerns are about a disaster or about the process of what you are developing?

Ms. ZIMMERMAN. It is about the disaster declaration guidance. But it is also to get a better understanding from our standpoint as to the impacts disasters bring to them and to be able to identify those unique characteristics and what it is we need to take into our understanding. What we are considering our first step is the declaration guidance. As we hear comments from tribal members about disaster programs, about FEMA programs, whether it is grants or other things, we are able to educate ourselves.

Senator BEGICH. I know in the 2015 budget you have about $1.5 million for regional office, I think it is enhanced tribal engagement and more activity under salaries and expenses. So in the 2016 budget that I know you are in the process, and it is hard to believe, right, that you are in that? But can you tell me, are you going to have enough information and detail, because it is just salaries and expenses, it doesn't tell us, at least me, enough of how you are going to do what you have just said plus more engagement that is necessary. Will that be more detailed or can you help me there understand that a little bit more?

Ms. ZIMMERMAN. I would have to get back to you.

Senator BEGICH. Will you do that for the record?

Ms. ZIMMERMAN. We can definitely get back for the record.

Senator BEGICH. What is your general comment of, and you may not have enough information yet because you are doing this kind of listening sessions process, of the nations, tribes and their ability to be prepared in the sense of preparedness? Where would you, if you had a one to ten scale, recognizing that different regions have higher capacity or lower capacity, what would you say the preparedness of our tribes are for emergency preparedness? And I say this coming from a city, as a former mayor, that we strived on this every day, because we would have to deal with these issues on a very regular basis. So what would your sense be now and, I am giving a hypothetical one to ten.

Ms. ZIMMERMAN. I am saying it probably would be low, at this point. Because a lot of it is new. It is something that they haven't really specifically worked in. And if they haven't had a disaster, even to be in the old program, to work through the State to get a disaster declaration. But it is something that I think is important—A lot of the sessions I went to I heard about how they want to learn about the incident command system, how we run disasters, to have plans, what that plan looks like and the templates for that.

Senator BEGICH. Will you engage them in training and those kinds of activities?

Ms. ZIMMERMAN. Yes.

Senator BEGICH. Is that part of the budgetary process that you will want to incorporate?

Ms. ZIMMERMAN. Right. Since 2002, we have offered a tribal government emergency management course out of our Emergency Management Institute in Emmitsburg. And we have had over 3,000 tribal members attend that over the last 12 years. So as we go, we continue to develop more training classes and to deliver it in the field. Additionally, when we do open up a joint field office, because there has been a disaster declaration, we have been specifically in North Dakota with the Minot flooding, and we were able to bring in and conduct training for tribes in disaster management.

Senator BEGICH. Last question, I know my time is up. But in the national disaster recovery framework that you have, have you incorporated tribal governments in that process yet?

Ms. ZIMMERMAN. Yes. We did from the start, from day one when we were rolling out. As I traveled the Country, rolling it out with a blank piece of paper, we said how we are going to develop the recovery framework so that we can build some consistency in how we do recover from disasters.

Senator BEGICH. Tribal or local governments, State government.

Ms. ZIMMERMAN. Right. And we had many tribal members participate in that across the Country.

Senator BEGICH. Thank you very much, Mr. Chairman.

The CHAIRMAN. Thank you.

Before we go to our second panel, I just want to get your comment on one thing. That is, my crack staff gave me information that over a four-year period, 2010, 2011, 2012 and 2013, tribal awards amounted to, on average, .2 percent. Point 2 percent of the disaster relief fund. That would indicate to me, and we haven't done the math, but it would indicate to me that there may be something in the program that is a deterrent for Indian Country to go to FEMA. Do you know of anything that would be a deterrent?

Ms. ZIMMERMAN. I do not. I would have to look at the disaster declarations that have impacted tribal areas and if there were tribes that did not come in and ask for assistance. It would depend on where the disaster and damages occurred.

The CHAIRMAN. Okay, that sounds good. I just want to thank you for being here, Elizabeth. There will probably be questions submitted in writing for you to respond to later on, but we have to get to panel two, and we want to thank you for the work you do and being here today. Thank you very much.

And now I will welcome our second panel. I think we have a good mix of tribal officials from across the Country. We have the Honorable J. Michael Chavarria, who is the Governor of the Santa Clara Pueblo of New Mexico. He will be followed by Ms. Ronda Metcalf, Secretary for the Sauk-Suiattle Tribe in Washington State. Next we are going to hear from Matt Gregory, Executive Director of Risk Management for the Choctaw Nation in Oklahoma. We will then hear from Ms. Mary David, Executive Vice President of Kawerak, Incorporated out of Nome Alaska. You have come a long way. Finally, we are going to hear from Jake Heflin, President and CEO of Tribal Emergency Management Association. Once they get started, we will start with you, Governor Chavarria.

I would like to remind folks, if you could, because there are five of you who will testify, try to keep it to five minutes if you can. Know that your full written testimony will be a part of the record. That will give us an opportunity to ask some questions.

So with that, you may start, Governor Chavarria.

### STATEMENT OF HON. J. MICHAEL CHAVARRIA, GOVERNOR, PUEBLO OF SANTA CLARA

Governor CHAVARRIA. [Greeting in Native tongue.] Thank you very much for this opportunity, Chairman Tester, Vice Chairman

Barrasso and members of the Committee, this opportunity to provide testimony on natural disasters in Indian Country.

My name is J. Michael Chavarria. I serve as Governor for Santa Clara Pueblo, which is located in North Central New Mexico.

In 2011, Santa Clara Pueblo was impacted by the Las Conchas Fire. This fire was very devastating, impacting 80 percent of our watershed, forests and our spiritual sanctuary. A huge part of our way of life has been destroyed.

Because Santa Clara Canyon was stripped of its vegetation, it has become a funnel, generating intense flooding, which puts the Pueblos at risk. The Pueblo has worked with the Corps of Engineers and in a recent report that they published, they identified the village of Santa Clara Pueblo as in imminent threat of flooding with extreme loss of life, risk there and the property of Santa Clara Pueblo. This flooding has wiped out the existing water control structures within the canyon, destroyed pristine native cutthroat trout fish habitat, impacted roads, culverts. But most importantly, this traditional cultural property is located within our spiritual sanctuary.

These floods have caused approximately $150 million of infrastructure damage. The Pueblo was requested to come up with $50 million as our cost match to these Presidential disaster declarations, an amount far beyond our capacity and capabilities. We will also be seeking a waiver from the President regarding these four disaster declarations on behalf of the Pueblo Santa Clara.

The Santa Clara Pueblo in 2011 had to go with the State of New Mexico as a sub-grantee because there were no amendments to the Robert T. Stafford Act that allow the tribes to go directly to the President. Overall, the ability to directly request for a Presidential disaster declaration has given the Pueblo greater control over its own disaster relief efforts. Further, the implementation of the National Disaster Recovery Framework, NDRF, by FEMA, which facilitates interagency collaboration, has been very helpful to the Pueblo, initiating a comprehensive and coordinated effort among the Federal family.

However, the current laws and regulations regarding disaster relief remain the product of a different time with the effect of slow delivery of critically needed resources to the Pueblo to be implemented in a timely manner. Broadly, the flood disaster relief framework remains tailored to one-time floods on the Mississippi River and thus are focused on short-term efforts. Given the increasing effects of climate change, disaster relief policies must be shifted to focus on long-term response.

Empowering tribes to directly request a Presidential disaster declaration is helpful. But standing alone, it does not fully address the need for quick funding response. For this reason, we recommend the creation of a BIA, Bureau of Indian Affairs, Emergency Response Fund. The idea behind this fund will be for the BIA to have significant funding that can be deployed over multiple years to address short and long-term disaster recovery and disaster mitigation needs.

This proposal could be taken even further by the creation of an emergency management department or division within the Bureau of Indian Affairs.

Mr. Chairman and members of the Committee, five minutes is not enough time to share our experiences with you all. I request that you hold a field hearing in New Mexico during the monsoon season, which is now, so that we can all have a meaningful dialogue and you can see first-hand the experience the Santa Clara Pueblo has engaged in. Of course, we can't do that, but there is much more we can share, if you can't come to New Mexico and see the situation first-hand.

I would like to close by thanking the Committee for the opportunity and thanking the many Federal agencies and officials that have worked long hours and continue to address our concerns for the imminent threat of flooding that exists there in New Mexico. One of the challenges, Mr. Chairman, is the tribe must meet a million dollar threshold if we are supposed to go direct. A lot of the tribes don't have a million dollars in infrastructure damages.

So we are requesting that we lower, through these field hearings or these processes, maybe lowering that threshold to $250,000, even $500,000. Because ultimately, you must be eligible through your preliminary damage assessment. Once you declare, FEMA starts to come out and do an assessment. If you don't meet that million dollar threshold, you are not eligible for Federal assistance.

And so implementing this NDRF has been very important to the Pueblo of Santa Clara as it brings all these existing authorities within the Federal Government to them in a timely manner and provides assistance to the Pueblo when it is needed. Not having to wait a year after a disaster to finally get some funds obligated through a project worksheet, because we are already behind that eight ball.

So Mr. Chairman, members of the Committee, as I mentioned, five minutes is not enough time to stress the issues and concerns. But I really appreciate the opportunity of being here today and I also stand for questions after the panel has presented their statements.

Thank you, Mr. Chairman.

[The prepared statement of Governor Chavarria follows:]

PREPARED STATEMENT OF HON. J. MICHAEL CHAVARRIA, GOVERNOR, PUEBLO OF SANTA CLARA

**Introduction.**

Thank you Chairman Tester, Vice Chairman Barrasso, and members of the Committee for this opportunity to provide testimony on the critically important topic of natural disasters in Indian Country. My name is J. Michael Chavarria, and I am the Governor of the Santa Clara Pueblo located in north-central New Mexico. Because of wildfires and subsequent intense flooding, the Santa Clara Pueblo has had four Presidential Disaster Declarations (or PDDs) in the last three years. Indeed, in a recent report, the Army Corps stated: "The Village of Santa Clara Pueblo is in imminent threat of large damaging floods with extreme life safety risk." My testimony (1) shares our experiences with disaster relief, and (2) urges the creation of a Bureau of Indian Affairs (BIA) Emergency Response Fund, among other recommendations.

**Tremendous Efforts of Many Federal Employees**

I would like to open by thanking the many individuals that we work with at the Federal Emergency Management Agency, the Army Corps of Engineers, the Bureau of Indian Affairs, the Bureau of Reclamation, the US Department of Agriculture and others for the long hours that they have committed to addressing what continues to be an existential threat to the Santa Clara Pueblo. Despite working with laws and regulations that can be cumbersome or just simply designed for very different emergencies, they continue to show commitment and determination, for which I and my people are truly grateful. There is work to be done and there are significant improvements to be made, but at Santa Clara we have hope that after suffering a terrible loss we can secure the safety of our community in the short term and its cultural and spiritual integrity and prosperity in the long-term.

**Need for a Policy Shift**

Santa Clara has had four Presidential Disaster Declarations. Two were secured by request of the State of New Mexico and two were secured by direct request of the Tribe after the Stafford Act was amended. Overall, the ability to directly request Presidential Disaster Declarations has given Santa Clara Pueblo greater control over our own disaster relief efforts. Further, the implementation of the National Disaster Recovery Framework (NDRF) by FEMA, which facilitates inter-agency collaboration, has been helpful to Santa Clara in assuring a comprehensive and coordinated effort among the Federal family. However, despite the hard work of many dedicated agency staff members, current laws and regulations regarding disaster relief remain a product of a different time, with the effect of still slowing the delivery of critically needed resources. Broadly, the flood disaster relief framework remains tailored to onetime floods on the Mississippi River and thus are focused on short-term efforts (and this not only refers to funding, but to how each contract is written and the expectations of the implementing policies). Given the realities of life in the southwestern United States and the increasing effects of climate change, disaster relief policies must be shifted to focus on long-term response such as addressing Santa Clara's post-fire, periodic flooding, which will remain a great hazard to our well-being for perhaps a decade, as the Santa Clara Canyon slowly recovers. Although significant progress has been made, more work remains to be done to ensure effective responses to natural disasters in Indian Country.

**Background**

In the summer of 2011, the Santa Clara Pueblo was devastated by the Las Conchas Fire, which was then the largest wildfire in New Mexico history. We estimate that over 16,000 acres of our forest lands were burned and, together with the lands we lost in the Oso Complex Fire of 1998 and the Cerro Grande Fire of 2000, 80 percent of our forests and a huge part of our heritage has been destroyed. None of the four fires we have faced in the past decade have originated on our lands, yet we have suffered severe consequences.

The Las Conchas fire also burned thousands of acres of our traditional lands outside our current reservation—including the lands of our origin, the P'opii Khanu, which are the forested headwaters of the Santa Clara Creek. The Santa Clara Creek drains the east side of the Jemez Mountains, delivering its waters to the Rio Grande near Española, NM. The Las Conchas burn scar within impacted 25.9 miles of Santa Clara Creek's upper watershed. The Pueblo owns almost the entire watershed, and the Tribal village is located on Santa Clara Creek's alluvial fan, where the Santa Clara Creek joins the Rio Grande.

Because Santa Clara Canyon has been stripped of its vegetation, the Pueblo has experienced severe flash flooding. All four Presidential Disaster Declarations have involved infrastructure damages stemming from catastrophic flash floods. Flooding has wiped out existing water control structures within the canyon, destroyed once-pristine native cutthroat fish habitat, impacted roads, taken away culverts, and damaged the traditional cultural properties of our sanctuary.

**Continued Threat of Catastrophic Floods**

As a result of the altered hydrology and Geomorphic changes, the Pueblo is in greater danger today of a catastrophic flood. Because of the severity of the burn, there has been dramatic reduction in infiltration rates in the burned area. This has resulted in a four-to-eight-fold increase in runoff and sediment/debris flow along the creek, substantially increasing the potential for widespread damage.

The graph below contains data for the Santa Clara Creek pre-fire and post-fire. As the graph indicates, the worst case scenario is a 100-year storm. For the Rio Grande Confluence, such a storm would have flooded 5,640 cubic feet per second (cfs) pre-fire and now, post-fire, would flood 21,450 cfs.

Table 1: Flow Results Summary (cubic feet per second, cfs)
Source: Fire Altered Hydrology for Santa Clara Creek/ USACE Technical Assistance Report

| LOCATION | CONDITION | 50% CHANCE (2-YR) | 10% CHANCE (10YR) | 1% CHANCE (100-YR) |
|---|---|---|---|---|
| Santa Clara Creek at Dip Crossing | Pre-fire | 300 | 1,900 | 5,000 |
| | Post-Fire | 2,650 | 8,500 | 20,300 |
| Santa Clara Creek at Rio Grande Confluence (Outlet) | Pre-fire | 350 | 2,260 | 5,640 |
| | Post-Fire | 3,100 | 8,900 | 21,450 |

## Lessons from our Disaster Relief Experiences

Because of our four Presidential Disaster Declarations, Santa Clara Pueblo has experience both as a sub-grantee and as a direct grantee. As you are aware, previously Presidential Disaster Declarations had to be requested through the states. For tribes, securing a state request for a Presidential Disaster Declaration could be difficult. New Mexico did, however, request such declarations on behalf of Santa Clara Pueblo on two occasions. Unfortunately, in these instances it took up to a year for the Pueblo to receive the requested disaster relief funds from the State, hampering our ability to provide urgently needed, immediate relief.

Amendments to the Stafford Act now allow tribes to directly request Presidential Disaster Declarations. The ability to become direct-grantees has given Santa Clara Pueblo greater ability to direct its own disaster relief efforts. Additionally, the NDRF has been enormously helpful in coordinating agency responses and providing a more collaborative and effective approach to disaster recovery.

The direct grantee process, however, is not without its challenges. It is a new process, and Santa Clara Pueblo has been the first tribe to utilize it in FEMA Region VI. For both the Pueblo and the Region, there is a lot of learning that has to take place. We have been going through that learning process with FEMA—in many ways we feel like we are path-finders for other tribes, should they be so unfortunate as to face the difficulties we have faced.

As a sub-grantee, receiving funds through the state, the tribe must match 12.5 percent and the state has the burden of administering the grant. As a direct grantee, the tribe's match is 25 percent, although this can be lowered to 10 percent once the per capita threshold is met. Additionally, as a direct grantee the tribe is responsible for the administrative costs associated with the grant, although the Pueblo receives 3.37 percent in administrative funding from FEMA. Tribes may also face challenges meeting the $1 million FEMA threshold. This threshold should be developed to coincide with tribes' financial resources and capacities, and tribal consortiums should be able to apply for relief in order to meet this threshold.

Santa Clara Pueblo, as a direct grantee, has seen smaller funded projects be funded very quickly by FEMA, but larger Project Worksheets still proceed through a time-consuming quality assurance/quality control process. This process is clearly important, but it greatly lengthens the review time, and yet it is very important to get these funds working when you face the situation Santa Clara faces, where the next disaster is inevitable, it is only a matter of when. Right now, we are in the New Mexico monsoon season. Every day we scan the skies and read the weather reports, fearing the worst and praying for the best. Receiving funds to support recover efforts prior to the seasonal impacts of monsoons is imperative in breaking the cycle of continued damage that has resulted in four Presidential Disaster Declarations for Santa Clara Pueblo. As our experiences demonstrate, in emergency situations project implementation is crucial to protecting lives, securing our community, and preventing repeated damage to key infrastructure.

The four Presidential Disaster Declarations have put a significant financial burden on the Pueblo as a small tribe. The matching funds requirements across four PDDs have drained the Pueblo's financials resources. Due to these tremendous financial responsibilities, the Pueblo has requested FEMA to combine the four PDD into one PDD so that the Pueblo is in a better position to meet the financial cost share responsibilities. This would allow the Pueblo the opportunity to get to the 90/10 cost share, using the per capita figures to get to that level. Right now we are only going to meet that threshold on one PDD, while the first two as a sub-grantee with the State will remain at 12.5 percent with remaining PDD as a direct grantee at 25 percent. These variations are challenges we must be aware of so that the

Pueblo properly allocates funds to be in a position to move forward with our obligations.

Finally, the administrative responsibility that comes along with being a direct grantee has challenged the Pueblo. We certainly have proven that we have the administrative capability but we had to learn through trial and error. As the changes to the Stafford Act allowing Tribes to request direct are promulgated, FEMA could be best served by implementing a training program that better communicate the regulatory requirements that come along with being a direct grantee. This would position the tribes nationwide to be better recipients of FEMA's help and this would also allow FEMA to become more familiar with the capabilities of tribal governments.

As the first tribe in Region 6 to receive direct funding, we know that we are involved in a learning process with our federal partners. Training and capacity building is needed on both sides of the federal-tribal partnership. Tribes need additional training to administer funds successfully and our federal partners could benefit from allowing tribes such as Santa Clara Pueblo to conduct training for tribal liaisons to help them become more familiar with working with tribal governments. Together we can work to build the capacity of both tribal and federal actors and to identify areas in which disaster relief policy can be adapted to better fit the circumstances of natural disasters in Indian Country.

**Emergency Response Fund**

Our experiences with disaster relief highlight the need for tribes to receive assistance as soon as possible following a natural disaster. Empowering tribes to directly request a Presidential Disaster Declaration can be helpful, but standing alone it does not fully address the need for quick funding. For this reason, we recommend the creation of a BIA Emergency Response Fund. The idea behind this fund would be for the BIA to have readily at hand significant funding that can be deployed over multiple years, if necessary, to address short- and long-term disaster recovery and disaster mitigation needs.

**Other Recommendations**

Santa Clara has a few other recommendations that range more widely than those set forth above:

*1. Appropriate necessary funds for implementation of Forest treatments as identified under the Tribal Forest Protection Act (TFPA).* The TFPA authorizes the Secretaries of Agriculture and Interior to give special consideration to tribally-proposed Stewardship Contracting or other projects on Forest Service or BLM land bordering or adjacent to Indian trust land in order to protect the Indian trust resources from fire, disease, or other threat coming off of that Forest Service or BLM land. These stewardship agreements are an important tool for fighting the ever-growing threat of wildfires in the West. Empowering tribal governments as caretakers to protect tribal lands by managing adjacent federal lands is a smart policy. Santa Clara urges the Committee to support the expansion of this program by both the Department of Agriculture and by the Department of the Interior.

*2. Implement funding for treatments, on and off the reservation, utilizing microsite of land management.* This would be done forgoing the NEPA process to quickly implement a plan of action of lesson the threat of catastrophic fires from encroaching upon our Trust Resources. Huge amounts of funds are used annually for fire suppression while those same funds could be used to implement Hazardous Fuels Reduction, Fuel Breaks etc. to lessen the financial responsibility of the Federal Government for fire suppression activities.

*3. Continue consultations with tribes regarding implementation of the Stafford Act amendments.* The Pueblo has been engaged with navigating a new system afforded by the amendments to the Robert T. Stafford Act. The opportunities also come with challenges-and education about the process is essential on both sides of the table as to properly protect the integrity of such responsibilities that come along as a Direct Grantee.

*4. In addition to creating an Emergency Management Fund within the BIA, create an Emergency Management Department (EMD).* The EMD would be responsible for protecting Trust Resources before, during and after emergency situations. Appropriations could be funneled through the 93–638 process which would allow the Tribes to use those funds as cost match to other Federal Authorities. This would allow the Tribes to be in a positon to meet the required cost match associated under each Authority dealing with a Presidential Disaster

Declaration, thus providing the protection of lives and community infrastructure from future impacts.

*5. Provide adequate funding to Fire Suppression Activities budgets.* Hazardous Fuels Reduction funding is impacted by the high costs "Mega Fires" that has become the new trend in wildfires, and reduces the ability of being able to proactively reduce or minimize the effects of wildfire on tribal forests. There are many programs that can reduce the risk of catastrophic wildland fires. These include but are not limited to: Collaborative Forest Landscape Restoration, Hazardous Fuels, and Federal and Cooperative Forest Health programs, Stewardship Contracting Authorities under the Tribal Forest Protection Act, State Fire Assistance, and others. Approaches to restoring fire-adapted ecosystems often require treatment or removal of excess fuels (e.g., through mechanical thinning, prescribed fire, or a combination of the two) that reduce tree densities in crowded forests, and the application of fire to promote the growth of native plants and reestablish desired vegetation and fuel conditions.

Thank you for your consideration of this testimony.

**Appendix: USACE Map**

Below is a Map created by the USACE contractor Tetra Tech indicating the potential flood inundation for potential flood events from 2 yr. thru 500 yr. flood events within the Santa Clara Pueblo Community.

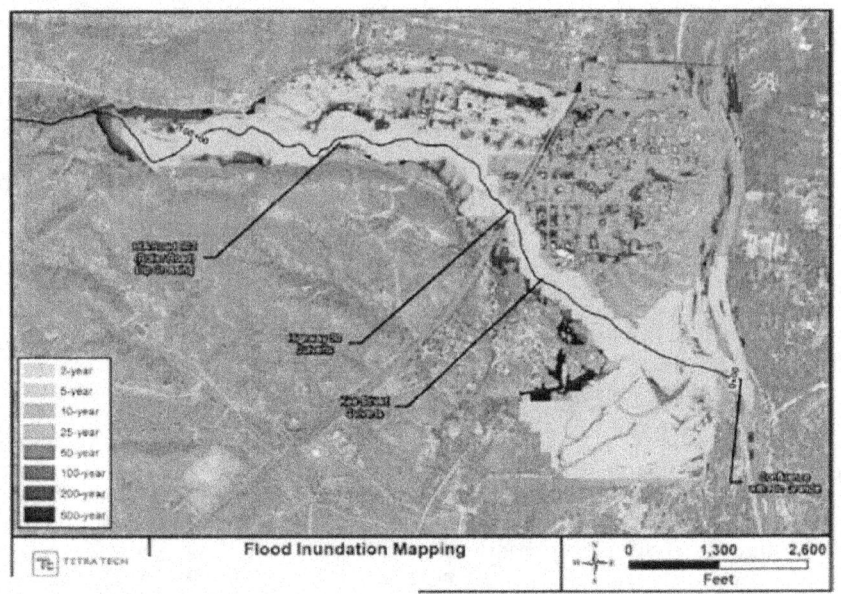

Initial flood inundation mapping based on the post-fire FLO-20 model simulations of the 2- through 500-year events. The long, straight boundaries at many locations result of the 150-foot grid elements in the FLO-20 model.

The CHAIRMAN. Thank you for your testimony, Governor.
Ms. Ronda Metcalf, you are up.

### STATEMENT OF HON. RONDA METCALF, SECRETARY, SAUK–SUIATTLE INDIAN TRIBE

Ms. METCALF. Thank you. Good afternoon, Chairman Tester and members of the Committee. My name is Ronda Metcalf.

Although I am going to say I am honored to be here, I have to say that it is sad for me to be here to have to give this testimony for my tribal members, the Sauk-Suiattle Indian Tribe. I am a council member and I am employed as the General Manager of the Tribe.

This is probably our first time in quite a while in appearing before a committee, so I wanted to provide some brief background about the Sauk-Suiattle Tribe. The tribe is located in the North Cascade Mountains of Washington State, just outside the town of Darrington. The tribe's reservation was established in 1985, including our reservation lands. The tribe currently is the beneficial owner of approximately, this is incorrect, because we just bought 100 acres of land, so we now own 200 acres of land. The tribe has approximately 225 enrolled members. The tribe does not have a gaming facility. Most of our tribal government revenue is from the tribe's small business and Federal grants.

On the morning of March 22, 2014, the deadliest mud disaster in United States history occurred in Oso, Washington. Our Vice Chairman, Kevin Lennon, was one of the first responders. He was there, he is a volunteer firefighter for District 24 of Darrington. And we lose Kevin on a daily basis, because he is a volunteer firefighter and rescuer. We did not see Kevin for the first eight days. So we do have a part in the town of Darrington.

This landslide engulfed 49 homes and was responsible for the death of 43. The last person's body was found last week, so we are very happy about that. It also dammed the Stillaguamish River, causing extensive flooding upstream, as well as blocking State Route 530. Actually, the mudslide destroyed Highway 530.

In destroying Highway 530, it also destroyed the infrastructure that went to the city of Darrington and the Sauk-Suiattle Indian Reservation, that being the phone lines disrupted phone service, internet service and everything that we need to use to survive on a daily basis. I think it is important to know that all the draw downs for funding from the BIA, Indian Health Services, come through the internet. That is the only way we get them.

Based on the tribe's experiences in dealing with the Oso disaster, I want to highlight a few points that are detailed in our written statement. First, FEMA needs to clarify its requirements for tribal emergency declarations. An emergency declaration is usually made during the immediate rescue phase of a disaster and allows for direct assistance from Federal personnel. That is the direct declaration that the tribal chairman and the council was trying to write. These are different than the requests for the Presidential disaster declaration, which triggers FEMA's public assistance and individual assistance program.

The FEMA staff could not provide clear guidance on what they required for tribal emergency declarations. It took 19 days, from March 27th to April 15th, 2014, for us to achieve an emergency declaration that FEMA would accept. The confusion and uncertainty resulted in delaying the tribe receiving assistance.

Second, FEMA must improve its coordination with tribes and charitable organizations, like the Red Cross. For example, FEMA requested that the tribe add additional staff to operate our tribally-owned convenience store to meet the needs of the first responders. The tribe was happy to assist in the rescue and recovery efforts in any way that we could, and readily agreed. FEMA represented to us that the tribe would be reimbursed for this additional payroll expense. Despite what the tribe was initially told, FEMA later informed us that these expenses were not reimbursable because the business was owned by the tribe.

We also experienced problems in dealing with the Red Cross. Although not a Federal agency, the Red Cross works closely with FEMA and gets reimbursed by FEMA for many of its responses costs. The tribe understands that the on-ground personnel in a disaster situation face significant challenges and pressures. This is all the more reason why FEMA must better coordinate with Indian tribes to provide accurate information and improved delivery of services.

Finally, the BIA and IHS should formalize their disaster response protocols and make emergency resources available for tribes for major disasters. The closure of State Route 530 severely impacted our tribe's members' ability to receive medical care from Arlington, Marysville and Everett and other locations. IHS wrote our chairman, suggesting that our tribal members take public county transportation to medical appointments, because it was a free service. When tribal members are sick, elderly and do not feel well, a difficult, more than 90 mile public bus trip each way is not an acceptable Federal response. A better approach would have been for IHS to provide medical staff or mobile health units to the reservation or provide funding for more patient transport of Indian patients affected by the disaster. We urge the Committee to explore with IHS, utilizing IHS's catastrophic health emergency fund, referred to as the CHEF fund, to pay for these types of costs.

In closing, the tribe would like to express its thanks to the other Indian tribes that provided us with assistance. The Nisqually Tribe sent us food and water, the Colville Tribes sent their emergency management team to assist us with the technical aspects of emergency management. And the Stillaguamish tribe provided us with some fuel cards for our tribal members.

That concludes my testimony. I would be happy to answer questions.

[The prepared statement of Ms. Metcalf follows:]

PREPARED STATEMENT OF HON. RONDA METCALF, SECRETARY, SAUK-SUIATTLE INDIAN TRIBE

Good afternoon, Chairman Tester, Vice Chairman Barrasso, and members of the Committee. My name is Ronda Metcalf and I am pleased to provide this testimony on behalf of the Sauk-Suiattle Indian Tribe (''Tribe'' or ''SSIT'') on responses to natural disasters in Indian country. I serve as the Tribal Council Secretary elect, and General Manager of the governmental administrative offices of the Tribe.

On behalf of the Honorable Norma A. Joseph, Chairwoman of the Tribe, I would like to express our appreciation to the Committee for holding this important hearing. We believe our Tribe's experience dealing with aftermath of the catastrophic mudslide in Oso, Washington, this past spring will be valuable to the Committee as it considers solutions to these issues.

As explained below, the Tribe has three main observations from its recent experiences. The first is the need for FEMA to clarify its requirements for tribal emergency declarations. Secondly, FEMA must improve its coordination with tribes and charitable organizations like the Red Cross to provide affected tribes with accurate information and reliable assistance. Finally, the Bureau of Indian Affairs (BIA) and the Indian Health Service (IHS) should formalize disaster response protocols and make emergency resources available when tribes are affected by major natural disasters like the Oso mudslide.

## Background on the SSIT

The Tribe was a signatory to the Point Elliot Treaty of 1855 as the Sah-ku-mehu. Our Homelands are located in the North Cascades, including the entire drainage area of the Stillaguamish, Sauk, Suiattle and Cascade Rivers. We have lands and businesses located within the Stillaguamish valley corridor. All the basic utilities that serve these areas come up through the Stillaguamish Valley. The Tribe's reservation was established in 1985 and is located about two miles into Skagit County along State Route 530 ("SR 530"), just outside the town of Darrington. There are approximately 20 homes, the tribal administrative offices, Health and Social Services and Tribal Police on the reservation. In our community all emergency services are provided on a cooperative basis by Snohomish County Fire District 24. Our Tribal Council Vice-Chair, Kevin Lenon, is a volunteer with the fire department and is ordinarily designated as the lead person in connection with any emergency.

Currently, the Tribe has over 225 members who reside on, off, or near the Tribe's reservation lands, as well as numerous members of other tribes. The Sauk-Suiattle Tribal Council is comprised of seven elected officials who make up the governing body of the Tribe. Including its reservation, the Tribe currently owns or is the beneficial owner of approximately 100 acres of land. We were canoe people, plying the swift waters of the Sauk, Suiattle, Stillaguamish, Cascade, and Skagit Rivers, and the Salish Sea. Hunting, fishing and gathering at usual and accustomed places we have utilized since time immemorial have been the Tribe's traditional sources of revenue, subsistence, and ceremonial needs.

## The OSO Mudslide

On the morning of March 22, 2014, the deadliest mudslide disaster in United States history occurred in Oso, Washington. This landslide engulfed 49 homes, was responsible for the deaths of 43 people and destroyed utility infrastructure. It also dammed a river, causing extensive flooding upstream as well as blocking SR 530, which is the main thoroughfare into and out of the town of Darrington. The town of Darrington is approximately 11 miles east of the mudslide epicenter and has a population of approximately 1,300.

With SR 530 being closed for an indefinite time, the socio-economic impact of the Oso mudslide to the Tribe and its members was severe and devastating in various ways. Please note that all socio-economic activities of the Tribe are tied to and conducted in the cities of Arlington, Marysville and Everett, Washington. This mudslide destroyed the vital communication infrastructure of the Tribe such as land and cell phones, and Internet service. Without phone or Internet service, tribal government operations largely came to a standstill and made the process of initiating emergency services nearly impossible.

From March 22, 2014, through June 1, 2014, the Tribe and its tribal members had to commute 92 miles each way to the town of Arlington using an alternate route. With high gasoline prices at nearly $4.00 dollars per gallon, the additional commute for tribal members to work or receive medical services in Arlington, Marysville and Everett was an extreme, day-to-day financial burden. Many of these household incomes are already under 200 percent below the poverty level.

In the immediate aftermath of the Oso mudslide, the Tribe requested assistance from many different federal agencies, including the BIA. The only immediate response we received was from the BIA's Puget Sound Agency. The acting agency superintendent and his staff came to the reservation first thing the following Monday to evaluate the Tribe's needs. All of our operating costs for the Tribe's governmental programs increased during the months of March, April, May, June. Those increases continue to affect the Tribe's budget today.

### 1. FEMA Must Clarify its Requirements for Tribal Emergency Declarations

Generally, tribes and states can make two types of declarations for FEMA assistance. The first is an emergency declaration, which is usually made during the immediate rescue phase of a disaster and allows for direct assistance from federal personnel. The second, more detailed declaration is a request for a Presidential Disaster Declaration (PDD), which triggers FEMA's Public Assistance and Individual Assistance programs. Congress amended the Stafford Act last year to allow tribes to request PDDs directly without going through state governments. FEMA is currently soliciting comments from tribes on draft guidance to implement the PDD request process.

Much less clear is what FEMA requires for emergency declarations. On March 27, 2014, Tribal Chairman Joseph made a Tribal Declaration of Emergency due to the impact of the SR 530 being closed for an indefinite time because one mile of the highway was under the mudslide. However, the assistance and instructions the Tribe received from FEMA were unclear as to the correct terminology to use in the emergency declaration. It took nineteen days, from March 27 to April 15, 2014, to achieve a declaration that FEMA would accept. This confusion and uncertainly resulted in delay in the Tribe receiving tangible assistance.

Washington State included the Tribe in its request for a PDD, which President Obama approved on April 2, 2014. The Tribe, however, remains unclear about FEMA's administrative requirements for emergency declarations.

Going forward, FEMA needs to formalize guidance on emergency declarations and how they relate to PDDs and ensure that field staff can provide tribes accurate guidance. More importantly, senior FEMA officials need to have this information and relay it directly to tribal leadership. The Tribe's size and lack of resources does not allow it to have the resources to maintain a full time emergency management department, so FEMA must be prepared to provide this information.

*2. FEMA Must Improve Its Coordination with Tribes and Charitable Organizations like the Red Cross*

In the weeks following the Oso mudslide, a number of problems arose because of either inaccurate information or lack of coordination on the part of FEMA or its partners.

For example, FEMA requested that the Tribe add additional staff to operate our tribally owned convenience store to meet the needs of the first responders. The Tribe was happy to assist in the rescue and recovery efforts in any way that it could and readily agreed. FEMA also represented to the Tribe that the Tribe would be reimbursed for this additional payroll expense. The Tribe also sold gasoline to emergency personnel at cost as a way of assisting the rescue and recovery efforts.

Despite what the Tribe was initially told, FEMA later informed the Tribe that the additional costs that the Tribe incurred at FEMA's request were not reimbursable because the business was owned by the Tribe. The Tribe relies upon revenue generated by retail and gasoline sales to consumers at its convenience store located on SR 530. As a result of the closure of SR 530, the Tribe lost revenue due to reduced sales which is ordinarily generated by tourist and other traffic. We are aware in prior disasters that FEMA field personnel have been confused about how trust property and tribally owned property would be treated for reimbursement purposes. The Tribe also understands that state governments are reimbursed when state employees work overtime to clear debris or otherwise respond to disasters. We still have not received a satisfactory explanation why these expenses are not reimbursable.

There was also inconsistency and confusion on the part of FEMA in providing transportation assistance. FEMA distributed gas cards to certain residents of the town of Darrington and yet told Tribal members that they were not eligible to receive this assistance. When the Tribe questioned FEMA about this discrepancy, we were told that they will come to the reservation and distribute the gas cards. FEMA staff, however, did not show up the day that they had promised.

In addition to FEMA, there was also inconsistency and confusion in the response on the part of charitable organizations such as the Red Cross. Although not a federal agency, the Red Cross receives reimbursement from FEMA for expenses it incurs in responding to disasters and coordinates closely with FEMA.

The Tribe was asked to accept gas vouchers given by the Red Cross and other charitable organizations, but the reimbursements of the gas vouchers took so long that our gasoline station incurred an $11,926.00 deficit in the month of April 2014. The store ran out of cash to pay the gasoline and other vendors who demanded cash upon delivery of goods and services. Again, these losses are apparently not reimbursable because the business is owned by the Tribe, or for other reasons that have not been explained. Similarly, the Stillaguamish Tribe donated gas cards to the Red Cross and FEMA to assist the population impacted and yet the tribal members of SSIT—who are also partners of the Stillaguamish Tribe—did not receive this assistance.

There were also logistical issues with food delivery. All donated food items were promptly distributed to assist the local food bank in the town of Darrington. On the other hand, it was not until May 2014, nearly a month and a half after the mudslide, that the Tribe finally received a shipment of donated food items from FEMA and the Red Cross. The food that ultimately arrived was several crates of spaghetti sauce which had past due expiration dates. Complicating matters was that the crates of food were infested with mice. This mouse infestation required the Tribe to close the buildings that the crates were stored in—one of which was the Tribe's day care facility—to conduct pest control. Again, these expenses were not reimbursable by FEMA.

In the end, neither our Tribe nor our tribal members could rely on FEMA's information. Some of our individual members received financial assistance in May 2014 but the promise of three months of assistance was never realized.

The Tribe understands that on-the-ground personnel in these disaster response situations face significant challenges and pressures. This is all the more reason why FEMA must better coordinate with Indian tribes to provide accurate information and improved delivery of services. FEMA must also provide closer supervision over organizations like the Red Cross to ensure that they are properly carrying out services for which they seek FEMA reimbursement.

When families are already struggling for assistance, they cannot be simply told by federal officials what they want to hear. They need to hear accurate information so that they do not have unreal hopes and expectations and can plan accordingly.

*3. The BIA and IHS Should Formalize Disaster Response Protocols and Make Emergency Resources Available when Needed*

Finally, the BIA and IHS should implement protocols and make changes to their programs to provide assistance to tribes when incidents like the Oso mudslide affect tribes and tribal members.

In the immediate aftermath of the mudslide, the Tribe's communications systems were severely impacted. On March 25, 2014, the BIA Regional Office in Portland promised the Tribe a mobile communication unit to improve the telecommunication of the tribe. To date, the SSIT communication systems such as land and cell phones, and Internet services are still not working properly. There are days that the Tribe has no landline, cell phone and Internet services. The BIA instructed the Tribe to provide it with a written description of needs following the mudslide. We provided this information to the BIA but have yet to see any action on those items.

The closure of SR 530 severely impacted our Tribal members' ability to receive medical care from Arlington, Marysville, Everett, and other locations that were not accessible via SR 530. IHS wrote to our Chairman suggesting that our members take public county transportation to travel for 60 miles from the reservation to Sedro Woolley to medical appointments because it was a free service. Not only was this not free, but it but it required tribal members to transfer buses several times in order to reach Mt. Vernon, Arlington, Marysville and Everett—another 60 miles. When tribal members are sick, elderly, and do not feel well, a more than 90 mile public bus trip each way is not an acceptable federal response.

A better approach would have been for IHS to provide medical staff or mobile health units to the reservation, or provide funding for more efficient private transport of Indian patients affected by these types of disasters. The Tribe urges the Committee to explore with IHS utilizing IHS's Catastrophic Health Emergency Fund, popularly referred to as the ''CHEF,'' to pay for these types of costs going forward.

In closing, the Tribe would like to express its thanks to the other Indian tribes that provided SSIT with assistance. The Nisqually Tribe sent food and water. The Colville Confederated Tribes sent some of their emergency management personnel to assist the Tribe on technical aspects of emergency management. As previously mentioned, the Stillaguamish Tribe provided our members with fuel assistance and other support.

This concludes my testimony. At this time, I would be happy to answer any questions that the members of the Committee may have.

The CHAIRMAN. Thank you for your testimony, Ronda.
Matt Gregory, from Choctaw.

### STATEMENT OF MATT GREGORY, EXECUTIVE DIRECTOR OF RISK MANAGEMENT, CHOCTAW NATION OF OKLAHOMA

Mr. GREGORY. Thank you.

In the past 13 years, I have watched the Choctaw Nation become far better prepared for disasters that keep hitting our people and our neighbors. But we have much more to do. And we need your help.

Today I want to highlight three points. First, the Stafford Act threshold of $1 million is too high for the disasters in much of impoverished, infrastructure-less Indian Country. Second, relative to size and challenges, Indian Country receives unfairly small share of disaster funds from DHS. Third, we need a GAO study to provide better information in disaster response, capabilities and resources in Indian Country.

The Choctaw Nation governmental responsibilities are daunting. Our boundaries cover ten and a half counties, 11,000 square miles, 230,000 people, and one-fifth of those are Choctaw members. The lives and families of our members are intertwined with those of our neighbors. Our government shares responsibilities with dozens of neighboring towns, city and county governments.

We know from the news that Southeastern Oklahoma is confronted each year by several natural disasters: tornadoes, ice storms, high winds, drought, wildfires, earthquakes. As we speak, we currently are under a flash flood watch in Southeastern Oklahoma. Tornadoes alone, between 1950 and 2014, hit Choctaw communities 336 times, with 48 deaths and $73 million in damages.

The Choctaw Nation's first instinct is to help. For example, when an EF3 tornado hit Tushka three years ago, killing two people and injuring 40, we immediately provided food, water and supplies and helped in cleanup and rebuilding. We do that every time an event occurs, big or small, Choctaw or not.

The tribal disaster assistance is absolutely vital in Indian Country, where insurance coverage is often not affordable and non-existent. In the Tushka tornado event, one-half the houses affected did not have home insurance. Additionally, the current premiums for home insurance have increased as much as 50 percent since 2011.

All of this can be very challenging. The good news is that with strategic mitigation projects, we have lessened the effects of disasters on our tribal members and the communities in which we reside.

We applaud your changes to the Stafford Act. They strengthen sovereignty and allow tribes like the Choctaw Nation to seek a disaster declaration directly from the President. But the Stafford Act needs further improvement. The $1 million in damages as a threshold for applying for a disaster declaration, this often does not work for a tribe which has small communities spread out over remote rural areas. As you know, a one size fits all, cookie cutter approach never works well in Indian Country, especially in Oklahoma, where tribes are poor and typically do not own utilities, roads and other infrastructure that, during a disaster, help a county or State reach the $1 million damage threshold.

I also ask your help in expanding opportunities for tribes for more direct Federal assistance for preparedness and mitigation projects. Over the last four years, Indian tribes have received just 1.3 percent of DHS grant funds. More tribal specific funding opportunities are needed.

Finally, very little information exists regarding preparedness, disaster response and recovery within American Indian and Alaska Native communities. We request that you utilize the GAO to study the homeland security and emergency management capabilities of tribes. The GAO report will help inform Federal decision-makers and assist tribal leaders and identify specific legislative changes that may be necessary.

In conclusion, we do not have all the answers. But we do want to be included in the discussion and help shape the solutions. FEMA and Homeland Security should broaden its dialogue with Indian tribes to develop and implement a disaster response policy that makes sense for all of Indian Country. The continued support of the Committee is critical to the success of the life and death emergency preparedness of Indian Country.

Thank you.

[The prepared statement of Mr. Gregory follows:]

PREPARED STATEMENT OF MATT GREGORY, EXECUTIVE DIRECTOR OF RISK MANAGEMENT, CHOCTAW NATION OF OKLAHOMA

Good Afternoon. Mr. Chairman, Members of the Committee, my name is Matt Gregory and I am the Executive Director of Risk Management for the Choctaw Nation of Oklahoma. On behalf of our Chief, the Honorable Gary Batton, I thank you for this opportunity to testify.

I am responsible to the Choctaw Nation for oversight of its Emergency Management Program. Our job is to ensure that the Choctaw Nation is prepared for, and ready to respond to, the next disaster. I've held this responsibility for 13 years, and have many years of experience in the fields of risk management, insurance and public safety. The Choctaw Nation has grown our emergency response program over the past 5 years and we expect that we will need to further expand our capabilities.

The Choctaw Nation jurisdictional boundaries cover a 10½ county-wide area in southeastern Oklahoma, including Bryan, Atoka, Coal, Pittsburg, Haskell, Latimer, LeFlore, Hughes, McCurtain, Choctaw, and Pushmataha counties. We are responsible for approximately 11,000 square miles. This mostly rural area has a Census 2010 population of 233,126. Of that, approximately 42,000 are Choctaw tribal members. The Choctaw Nation shares governmental responsibilities with various local units of government. Because of our checkerboard land ownership and the generations of non-members who now live among tribal citizens in our communities, our challenges are somewhat different from tribal governments who exercise jurisdiction over an intact reservation land base. Our tribal government responsibilities are necessarily intertwined with the governmental responsibilities of our neighboring towns, cities, and counties.

Along with our neighbors, the Choctaw Nation of Oklahoma usually is confronted by several natural disasters each year; including tornadoes, ice storms, high winds, extreme cold, hail storms, lightning, life-threatening heat, drought, wildfires, earthquakes, hazardous material releases, dam failures, and transportation accidents. In 2007, Oklahoma endured nine separate federally-declared disasters.

Throughout our history the Choctaw Nation has been plagued by significant disasters that disrupt our lives. According to the National Climatic Data Center, between 1950 and 2014, Choctaw Nation communities experienced 336 tornado events, with 48 deaths, and a total of $73 million in damages. In the last decade alone, Choctaw Nation communities lived through more than 1,450 events from all hazards and suffered damage totaling nearly $37 million, half of which was associated with 16 ice storms.

The 2007 winter ice storm had a significant impact on the citizens of Pittsburg and surrounding counties. 28,399 power outages were reported lasting for approximately two weeks. The Choctaw Nation responded immediately and worked with city, county, and state agencies to help those in need. Some of our activities included:

- Renting and placing generators in McAlester, Crowder, and Stigler at Community Centers used as shelters;
- Supplying water, food, toiletries, tarps, batteries, flashlights, lamp oil, and many other necessities to our tribal members and other citizens in the affected areas; and
- Collaborating with the National Guard to place a generator at our Travel Plaza which we opened to allow responding emergency vehicles to fuel up and get supplies.

In April 2011 an EF3 tornado (winds measuring between 136–165 mph) struck the town of Tushka, just 26 miles from our Choctaw Tribal Headquarters, killing two people and injuring 40. The Choctaw Nation had many tribal members, employees, and neighbors deeply affected by this storm. The Choctaw Nation again responded immediately and had support on the ground within hours after the storm hit. At one point there were 100+ volunteers working in the area. Some of the activities included:

- Operating a feeding station at the Command Center for volunteer workers and displaced citizens;

- Delivering food, water, and basic necessities to several distribution points within the community;
- Opening the Atoka Community Center as a shelter and access point for tribal members needing services; and
- Setting up a first aid center for injured citizens and workers.

I want to note that a survey after the tornado indicated that nearly one-half of the residents of Tushka did not have property insurance coverage. We found that after that disaster, the cost of insurance became even more expensive, increasing by as much as 50 percent. The growing lack of insurance coverage makes the Choctaw Nation's disaster assistance all the more vital.

The Choctaw Nation has also responded to disasters like flooding events, microbursts, and winter storms. Our most recent response was to the winter ice storm that hit Choctaw, McCurtain, Leflore, and Pushmataha counties. During this event we performed the following activities:

- Renting and placing generators in Hugo and Antlers at Community Centers used as shelters;
- Renting and placing generators in Bethel and Smithville at Community Centers used as warming stations and water distribution sites;
- Supplying water, food, toiletries, tarps, batteries, flashlights, lamp oil, and many other necessities to our tribal members and other citizens in the affected areas; and
- Coordinating with the Red Cross and the Southern Baptist Disaster Relief to cook and deliver meals to several shelters and feeding stations.

The Choctaw Nation of Oklahoma has responded to disasters outside our geographical boundaries as well. All citizens of Oklahoma are faced with these various disasters and the leadership of the Choctaw Nation of Oklahoma understands that unity in these times is critical to recovering from a disaster. After the tornado struck Chickasaw communities in Moore, Oklahoma in 2013, the Choctaw Nation responded with equipment, personnel, and financial resources to assist in cleanup and recovery. Disasters affect every aspect of life, and require a wide variety of responses (for example, one of the many things we did was deliver chicken feed in Moore to keep flocks alive in the days after the tornado destroyed their community). For its efforts in Moore, the Choctaw Nation was honored to receive the "Doing the Most Good" award from the Salvation Army, which is one of many great organizations with whom we cooperate in disaster relief.

The Choctaw Nation considers itself blessed to have resources available to assist our tribal members and neighbors during these disasters. In 2010 the Choctaw Nation received FEMA approval of our tribally adopted Tribal Multi-Hazard Mitigation Plan. We are currently working on updating this plan for resubmittal to FEMA. In 2012 we developed our Choctaw Nation Emergency Response Plan and established our Choctaw Nation Emergency Response Team. The Choctaw Nation currently utilizes the National Incident Management System and maintains current compliance with the program.

In 2012 the Nation hired a full time Emergency Manager and began to expand the development of the program. As of July this year the Nation has developed a joint Continuity of Operations/Continuity of Government or COO/COG plan, emergency communications plan, and is updating our Emergency Operations Plan or EOP. In addition the Nation will be developing several other plans to meet our needs and FEMA requirements (e.g., warning notification, public assistance administration, donation/volunteer management, other needs assistance, strategic development, and debris management).

In addition, the Choctaw Nation is also working closely with the State of Oklahoma and FEMA on a pilot project through the Emergency Management Accreditation Program, and we hope to be the first Tribe in the Nation to receive this accreditation. The Choctaw Nation has also been working on a project with the State and several Voluntary Organizations Active in Disasters or VOAD groups to ensure that the needs of children are met after a disaster strikes. In addition, the Choctaw Nation has been coordinating with the State to identify points of distribution for supplies in an effort to consolidate resources and coordinate more effective disaster response.

The Choctaw Nation is an active member of the Oklahoma Emergency Management Association (OEMA) and of the Inter-Tribal Emergency Management Coalition (ITEMC). ITEMC was developed to allow tribes to coordinate and share information regarding disaster response and preparedness activities. ITEMC has worked very closely with the State of Oklahoma and FEMA Region VI to bring training opportunities and vital information to the tribes regarding hazard mitigation and preparedness activities.

Planning efforts are very important and are vital to our success but we also realize the need for improvements through mitigation activities. The Choctaw Nation has completed several mitigation projects, including the following activities:

- Installed generators at several critical facilities;
- Developed a public information campaign;
- Implemented a storm shelter/safe room program and funded 1,136 shelters for elder and special needs tribal members;
- Purchased equipment for the delivery of supplies;
- Established a GIS department;
- Developed an EOP and response team;
- Secured equipment for our Public Safety division for disaster response; and
- Secured an off-site solution for data backup and recovery.

The Office of Emergency Management and the Emergency Management Program for the Choctaw Nation remains active in times when there are no disasters. Much of our effort focuses on the preparedness and capacity of the Tribe to recover from a disaster. Our vast coverage area can be a challenge but with strategic mitigation projects we hope to lessen the effects of a disaster on our tribal members and the communities in which we reside. As we move forward we hope to complete the following mitigation measures:

- Purchasing and installing generators at all of our Community Centers;
- Purchasing and installing generators at all of our Travel Plazas;
- Building multiple warehouses in specific locations for the quick disbursement of water and supplies;
- Building a hardened Emergency Operations Center;
- Purchasing a mass notification system to communicate with our employees and tribal members during a disaster or emergency situation; and
- Creating an arbor program to help mitigate falling tree limbs on power lines during winter events.

These are just a few of the new measures that will be in our Hazard Mitigation Plan and of course will depend on available funding through the Tribe and state and federal funding sources. Federal grant programs like PDM (Pre-Disaster Mitigation) and HMGP (Hazard Mitigation Grant Program) are critical to the success of any mitigation strategy and the Tribe is thankful for the opportunity to apply for these resources. We applaud the recent changes to the Stafford Act which strengthen the sovereignty of tribal governments and allow a Tribe like the Choctaw Nation to seek a disaster declaration directly from the President of the United States.

As we work with you and the Administration to implement our Stafford Act authority, there are some issues that may require further refinement. For example, the Stafford Act set $1 million in damage as its threshold for applying for a declaration. This may not work well for a Tribe like the Choctaw Nation, with small communities spread out over a wide rural area. A tornado can wipe out a small impoverished town of 30 homes and not meet the $1 million damage threshold. However, for the 30 families in that community, the devastation is overwhelming and the destruction is total. A one-size-fits-all, cookie-cutter approach never works very well in Indian Country, especially in Oklahoma, where tribes typically do not own utilities, roads, or other infrastructure that during a disaster help a county or state reach the $1 million damage threshold.

When the Choctaw Nation, as well as other tribes, responds to a disaster we are responding to the entire community not just our tribal members. This creates a list of other concerns with our new Stafford Act authority:

- If the State is not awarded a declaration but our Tribe is, can a county come to our Tribe for reimbursement of its costs related to the disaster?
- If the State and our Tribe or several tribes are awarded a declaration, how is that funding allocated?
- If our Tribe responds to the entire community are the costs related to non-tribal response efforts eligible for reimbursement?

These are just a few of the many unknowns regarding the changes to the Stafford Act. We do support changes to policy that strengthen tribal sovereignty and are committed to working with you to make these changes actually work in Indian Country.

We do not have all of the answers. But we do want to be included in the discussion and an opportunity to help shape some of the recommended solutions. We need the help of this Committee to persuade FEMA to open up a constructive dialogue with all Indian tribes to develop and implement a disaster response policy that makes sense for all of Indian Country. These answers need to come quickly. We are faced with a number of disasters throughout the year, and without quick and specific direction, our new-found Stafford Act authority lacks some practical effect.

We would ask your help in expanding the opportunities for tribes to receive direct federal assistance for preparedness and mitigation projects. These capacity-building opportunities are critical to the recovery of any community, especially tribal communities. Over the last four years, Indian tribes have received just 1.3 percent of the U.S. Department of Homeland Security grant funds available for preparedness and capacity building. Tribal specific funding opportunities would assist Indian tribes to better prepare for and recover from disasters.

Currently very little if any information exists regarding preparedness response and recovery within American Indian or Alaska Native tribal communities. We know far too little about the existing disaster-response capacity, or lack thereof, of tribal governments. We would request that Congress utilize the Government Accountability Office (GAO) to study the homeland security and emergency management capabilities of tribal governments. A GAO report may help inform federal decision-makers about the challenges of disaster response and recovery in Indian Country and also assist tribal leaders as we apply federal policies and opportunities to the needs we must meet in Indian Country. Perhaps that GAO report could also identify specific legislative changes that may be necessary to make the Stafford Act work more effectively in Indian Country.

Finally, we ask that the Committee urge FEMA and the Department of Homeland Security to include a larger presence of tribal representation on federal committees engaged in disaster response and recovery. Tribal representation from a variety of tribes should be required on committees such as Federal Incident Management Teams, FEMA National Advisory Council, and the FEMA Floodplain Management Council. The most useful understanding of tribal disaster response operations will come from those who deal with these situations on a daily basis.

Again, we are honored by this opportunity to testify and thank you for it. We appreciate the Committee's leadership and commitment to Indian Country and our needs in response to disaster situations. The Choctaw Nation is committed to continuing this dialogue and to better preparing our people to respond to and recover from disasters. Your continued support in these matters is critical to the success of emergency preparedness in Indian Country.

The CHAIRMAN. Thank you for your testimony, Mr. Gregory.

All the way from Nome, we have Mary David. The floor is yours.

## STATEMENT OF MARY DAVID, EXECUTIVE VICE PRESIDENT, KAWERAK, INC.

Ms. DAVID. Good afternoon. Thank you for giving me the opportunity today to testify.

I work for Kawerak, Incorporated, as the Executive Vice President. Our corporation represents 20 tribes in 16 communities. All of our communities are located along the sea coast or along the shores of rivers.

Last November, the President declared a disaster in Alaska for areas affected by severe storms, straight line winds and flooding. Several communities in the Bering Straits region were impacted by these storms. With these storms happening more often and more severely, coastal erosion seems to be happening quicker and more often. Shaktoolik, Shishmaref and Unalakleet were identified by the Immediate Action Work Group as three of six communities identified as imminently threatened. The 2009 GAO report included Golovin, St. Michael, and Teller. These threats to life and property still exist today, and are getting worse.

Stebbins, Alaska is not one of the villages listed, but due to last November's storms it was hit by a surge of waves that overflowed and flooded the community. FEMA needs to speed up the response and recovery process and go out to the communities as soon as possible after a known disaster occurs to also help individuals and let them be aware of what access they provide.

Access to emergency funds are also needed immediately to address life and safety issues such as obtaining heating fuel, safe drinking water, food, clothing, shelter and communication. Other response agencies, such as the Alaska Red Cross, local regional health and tribal organizations and other volunteers responded faster to Stebbins than the Federal and State government agencies did.

There is a lack of understanding by Federal agencies and personnel regarding the unique living situation of remote Alaska and the challenges that rural residents experience on a daily basis. Remote Alaska has no highways, there are no docks, no ports, no railroads connecting communities with other hub communities or even here to the lower 48. The only access is via barge from June 1st to September 30th and only by air when the weather is navigable.

In Stebbins, four homes were damaged and several homes had water damage inside the home. When disaster occurs, the time it takes to get back to normalcy can take six months to a year and oftentimes longer due to the challenges that exist in the wait time that it takes for supplies to arrive and repair to occur, due to our very, very short construction season.

Evacuation shelters supply the necessities and alternative evacuation routes are needed in more vulnerable communities. Preventive measures to slow the effects of erosion and flooding are needed while communities plan for long-term solutions. For the communities that are better off may be relocating they are placed in a catch-22 situation. Efforts to prevent and protect the existing village only prolongs the relocation efforts by reducing the urgency to move. Although tribes can declare a disaster to FEMA, the non-Federal cost share match is an issue. The Bering Straits tribes do not have available savings. They do not have industry services, such as gaming or mineral or revenue sources to meet that cost share match.

So in Kewarak's viewpoint, it is actually a detriment to the tribe if they bypass the State and declare a disaster to FEMA. Our Federal, State and local and tribal governments are all ill-prepared for both the natural disasters that we have already experienced and the potential future and natural and manmade disasters in the future in our region.

Not only is there a lack of a lead agency spearheading comprehensive efforts to prevent, mitigate and respond to disasters, there is a lack of coordination among the agencies that are tasked with carrying out the splintered components of these efforts. The Stafford Act addresses the response effort when disaster happens, which is important. But due to changing climate conditions, changing sea ice conditions and melting permafrost and the extreme variations in the weather, our communities are in imminent danger and preventive measures are needed. No person in the most developed country in the world should be subject to threats of loss of life due to conditions that can be mitigated by governmental action.

The United States provides humanitarian efforts to other countries, oftentimes spending millions of dollars on aid. Our local populations may be small, but we are impacted just the same when a disaster happens. We still deserve support and relief, similar to when a disaster occurs in other countries or even in lower 48 coastal communities. The U.S. is an Arctic nation and has an obligation to assert its sovereign authority and protect national interests. With the authority comes responsibility for disaster prevention, mitigation and response, especially in an area such as the Bering Straits region, which is extremely remote and exposed to international ocean traffic.

Thank you for giving me the opportunity to testify on this important issue.

[The prepared statement of Ms. David follows:]

PREPARED STATEMENT OF MARY DAVID, EXECUTIVE VICE PRESIDENT, KAWERAK, INC.

Chairman Tester, and esteemed members, thank you for giving me the opportunity to submit written testimony on the issue of responding to natural disasters in Indian country. My name is Mary David, and I'm the Executive Vice President of Kawerak, Inc. I was born, raised and live in Nome, Alaska. I am a tribal member of Nome Eskimo Community, I have a bachelors degree in Social Work from the University of Alaska, Anchorage and a Master of Public Administration from the University of New Mexico, Albuquerque, New Mexico.

Our environment is changing at an unprecedented rate. When the severe fall storms hit our region last November, 2013, several of our communities were impacted which brought to our attention areas that need improvement. Besides natural disasters, we are also threatened by potential manmade disasters due to increased ship traffic through the Bering Strait.

Kawerak is the tribal consortium in the Bering Strait region of Alaska, an area with 20 federally recognized tribes and 16 communities. The region is not connected to the rest of Alaska by roads, and 14 of the 15 communities are not accessible by road to the hub community of Nome. Primary access year round is by air service, with small commuter planes and gravel runways in most of the villages. The ocean freezes over the winter and barge services ends; air transportation for freight is thus higher in the winter as it must be flown in. All of the communities in the Bering Strait Region are located on the sea coast or shores of rivers. Our service area is approximately 26,000 square miles or roughly the size of West Virginia. The region's population is about 9,000 people, of which roughly 75 percent are Alaska Native (Inupiaq, Siberian Yupik and Yupik decent).

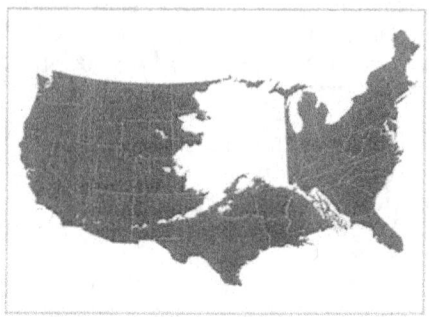

We are the first people to know when change is happening in our environment. The Inupiaq, Siberian Yupik and Yupik people have been in the Bering Strait region hunting and gathering from the land and sea since time immemorial. The marine life (pacific walrus, bow head whales, beluga whales, ice seals, polar bears, fish, ocean plants, sea urchins and sea birds) are vital and important sources of food. The impacts of global climate change, severe arctic storms and arctic shipping on marine life is of high concern due to our reliance on these food sources.

We notice a change in our environment. Our hunters are having to go further out to find walrus or oogruk (bearded seals). This may be due to a number of factors: noise, change in current pattern, weather, and ice conditions. Ice is a vital element to our survival and its condition has changed. Local experts have noticed that the ice is less stable, thinner, softer and melts more quickly in the spring. Our sea level is also rising. Places where people use to gather fish among the rocks are now inaccessible and where seals once hauled out on Savoonga, Alaska it is now underwater and unused. We have also noticed different species of animals in our region. The Steller sea lion, once seen during the summer months has recently been documented in the Bering Strait region into December and humpback whales now are seen with seasonal regularity north of Bering Strait and have even recently been documented in the north eastern Chukchi Sea. Additionally, different plant and animal life are being seen in locations where they have never been seen before. The Hanasaki king crab, *Parlithodes brevipes,* arrived to U.S. waters for the first time when it was pulled from a subsistence crab hole through the sea ice at Little Diomede during the spring 2003. Since that time, the Hanasaki crab is a common species harvested near Saint Lawrence Island. Several egg-bearing females were harvested and suggest that this unusual visitor is now a new part of the Bering Strait ecosystem.

Changes to our environment can be characterized by an increase in surface temperatures, changes to precipitation rates, erosion rates, decrease in sea ice coverage all stemming from climate change. (Progress Report, Inuit Circumpolar Conference, 2014) Severe "super" storms seem to occur more frequently and more severely. Hurricane force winds can hit our communities and can knock out power lines, cause storm surges, create tidal flooding, and impact service delivery and flights.

The photo is the roof of my neighbor's house due to wind damage sustained last November 2013. The photo shows the force of the wind during this super storm.

Last November 2013, the President declared a disaster in Alaska for areas affected by severe storms, straight-line winds, and flooding. There were several communities in the Bering Strait region that were impacted by a series of storms that affected western Alaska. The storm damage resulted from coastal flooding due to the storm surge and strong winds.

Kawerak has a Natural Resources division, which plays a key role in compiling Traditional Ecological Knowledge. Through our Social Science program, hundreds of hunters and gatherers (who have lived their whole lives observing the environment) provided data on the many changes they have witnessed, such as a rise in sea level, later freeze up and thinner ice, permafrost melting, changes in weather patterns, and shorter winters, more rain, and hotter summers. Absent the physical protections of landfast ice (which act as a seawall), there is more damage from severe fall and early winter storms. Several of our communities are experiencing rapid erosion of their shorelines, and may be better off being relocated.

The impacts from the storm may also be due in part from the lack of permafrost (permanently frozen subsoil), that holds our land together. With rising temperatures it has led to the thawing of the permafrost. When storms occur it erodes the shoreline and riverbanks much more easily due to its weakened state. The following are recent photos from the community of Teller, Alaska depicting erosion damage near their cemetery. As reported in a conversation with Tim Wolforth, with the Alaska Army National Guard, on a recent trip to Teller, local resident Joe Garnie informed him the edge near the cemetery has eroded about 20 feet recently. The next "big" storm or subsequent storms, where the crack in the ground is located, is potentially where more erosion could occur and expose graves.

Looking southwest away from Teller. Cemetery edge on left. Looking straight into the "slump zone" that is full of cracks in the ground, and is slanting down towards the beach.

Looking northeast towards Teller. The sunny day made capturing a good photograph in the shadows difficult. The overhanging top of the land can be seen in the upper right. Clumps of topsoil from the upper slumping zone are present down on the beach.

Photos and photo captions taken by: Tom Wolforth, Cultural Resource Manager and Tribal Liaison Alaska Army National Guard; Teller Visit: June 17, 2014

Erosion can be gradual or extreme with each fall/winter storm event. With the storms happening more often and more severely, coastal erosion seems to be happening quicker. Under Governor Palin, a Climate Change Sub-Cabinet was established which then convened the Immediate Action Work Group (IAWG) comprised of federal, state and local officials to come up with ways to protect Alaska's most at-risk communities. Shaktoolik, Shishmaref and Unalakleet (within the Bering Strait's region) were identified by the Immediate Action Work Group as three of six communities identified as imminently threatened. The 2009 Government Accountability Office Report to Congressional Requesters on villages threatened by flooding and erosion, identified Golovin, St. Michael, and Teller as imminently threatened by flooding and erosion, in addition to Shaktoolik, Shishmaref and Unalakleet. These threats to life and property still exist today, and are getting worse.

Stebbins, Alaska is not one of the villages listed, but due to last November's fall storm it was hit by high surge waves that overflowed and flooded the community. Stebbins is located on the northwest coast of St. Michael Island, on Norton Sound. It lies 8 miles north of St. Michael and 120 miles southeast of Nome. Currently the population is estimated at 572. Although the State Emergency Coordination Center provided advance warning of the storm, the community did not expect the magnitude of the storm and the potential impact of it, and therefore was not adequately prepared to respond to it.

Stebbins, Alaska flooding photos – November 2013

FEMA needs to speed up the response and recovery process, and should go out to the communities as soon as possible after a known disaster to see its impacts before the clean-up has begun. Also, it is hard for individuals and families to access assistance because of not knowing what is available; making a presence soon after a storm would help those in need. The tribes own limited resources were used to help meet immediate needs after the disaster. Access to emergency funds are needed immediately to address life and safety issues such as obtaining heating fuel, safe drinking water, food, clothing, shelter and communication. Other response agencies, such as the Alaska Red Cross, local regional health and tribal organizations and other volunteers responded much faster to Stebbins than the federal and state government agencies did.

There is a lack of understanding by federal agencies and personnel regarding the unique living situation of remote Alaska and the challenges rural residents experience on a daily basis. In remote Alaska there are no highways, no docks or ports, and no railways connecting most communities with other hub communities or the lower 48. The only access is via barge from June 1st through September 30th and by air service all year when the weather is navigable. Home owners do not have a Home Depot to go to and if substantial damage is done, they often are not repaired for months, sometimes years. Also, the affects of a storm are not always known or visible until the following spring. If a storm occurs late in the year, it is difficult to assess damages and to meet the timeframes for qualifying for assistance.

Nome, Alaska is the hub community in the region. It is 500 air miles from Anchorage and only has two daily Alaska Airline flights in/out of the city. Many goods and services (such as food, equipment, and building supplies) have to be flown in or barged in during the summer months. With Stebbins, the flood happened last November and work on cleaning the debris from the community is occurring this summer. In Stebbins, four (4) houses were damaged and several homes had water damage inside the home. The outside of these homes look good, but the inside water damage is difficult to clean and it is taking many months to make them livable again.

We are experiencing a housing shortage in Nome, and in the rural villages it may be worse. Several families may live together in one house. When disasters occur, the time it takes to get back to normalcy may take from six months to a year and often times longer due to the challenges that exist and the timeframe one has to wait for supplies to arrive and repair to occur during our short construction season.

Evacuation shelters (supplied with necessities) and alternative evacuation routes are needed in the more vulnerable communities. Preventative measures to slow the effects of erosion and flooding are needed while communities plan for long term solutions. For those communities who may be better off relocating, they are placed in a Catch-22 situation. Efforts to prevent and protect the existing village only prolongs the relocation efforts by thus reducing the urgency to move.

Our federal, state, local and tribal governments are ill-prepared for both the natural disasters that we have already experienced and the potential future natural and man-made disasters in our region. Not only is there a lack of a lead agency spearheading comprehensive efforts to prevent, mitigate, and respond to disasters, there is a lack of coordination among the agencies that are tasked with carrying out the splintered components of these efforts. In addition, many of our communities/tribes do not have response equipment or assets to assist or support in a disaster. General Manager Matt Melton with Alaska Chadux stated in the July 24th issue of the Nome Nugget Newspaper that ''In a real response[such as an oil spill response], we would bring in 50 to 100 people'', this does not include Coast Guard or DEC personnel. He further stated, ''In a small community like Teller, a large influx of people responding to a spill would stretch the community's capabilities. Plans need to be in place to supply the workers with food, places to rest and sleep after 12 hour shifts.''

Our communities alone do not have the resources and the finances to address erosion problems on their own (there are numerous regulations, different studies and environmental documents needed). The Immediate Action Work Group coordinated effort was successful for the six communities it identified as imminently threatened. By the end of 2009, through their efforts Shaktoolik, Shishmaref and Unalakleet had Comprehensive Emergency Plans completed and the training to execute the plans (what is needed is the continued effort to hold drills annually). There has been slow progress with other communities in getting required FEMA plans completed or erosion issues addressed since the IAWG work ended around 2011. The table below lists each community in the Bering Strait Region, population, information on who has completed a Hazard Mitigation Plan (HMP), emergency operation plan (EOP) and if the community has a search and rescue group and an established volunteer fire group:

| Communities | Population | Completed HMP | Completed EOP | SCERP* | Search & Rescue | Emergency Equipment | Established Volunteer Fire Group | VPSO* |
|---|---|---|---|---|---|---|---|---|
| Brevig Mission | 326 | No | No | No | Yes | No | No | 2 VPSOs |
| Diomede | 110 | No | No | No | No | No | No | Vacant |
| Elim | 294 | No | No | No | Yes | No | No | Vacant |
| Gambell | 643 | Yes | No | No | Yes | No | Yes | VPSO |
| Golovin | 154 | Yes | No | No | Yes | No | Yes | VPSO |
| Koyuk | 368 | No | No | No | Yes | No | Yes | VPSO |
| Nome | 3,695 | Yes | Yes | No | Yes | Yes | Yes | VPSO |
| Savoonga | 712 | Yes | No | No | Yes | No | Yes | Vacant |
| Shaktoolik | 214 | Yes | No | No | Yes | No | Yes | Vacant |
| Shishmaref | 615 | Yes | Yes | No | Yes | No | Yes | VPSO |
| St. Michael | 446 | No | No | No | Yes | No | Yes | Vacant |
| Stebbins | 612 | No | No | No | Yes | No | no | Vacant |
| Teller | 258 | No | No | No | Yes | No | No | Vacant |
| Unalakleet | 727 | Yes | Yes | No | Yes | No | Yes | 2 VPSOs |
| Wales | 136 | No | No | No | Yes | No | Yes | Vacant |
| White Mountain | 224 | No | No | Yes | Yes | No | Yes | VPSO |

[Shaktoolik, Alaska also has completed a draft – Climate Change Adaptation for At-Risk Community Adaptation Plan. Kawerak was awarded $200,000 to create tribal transportation safety management plans for the 16 tribes in KTP consortium. *SCERP – Small Community Emergency Response Plan; VPSO-Village Public Safety Officer]

We recommend funding to reinvigorate the IAWG, and a commitment from the current Governor to reinstate the working group. The importance and continued need of such a committee to address the flood and erosion threats that our communities continue to face is vitally important. This was an exemplary model of coordinating State, Federal and local leaders to prioritize projects, coordinate resources and implement projects. The IAWG was an effective Committee that placed upper level staff of agencies and organizations in an arena that allowed for information sharing and important dialogue. The IAWG made recommendations to the State, the U.S. Army Corps of Engineers, and other agencies to fund mitigation projects that addressed immediate threats from flooding and erosion. The IAWG also allowed members and leaders from communities that are threatened to share their threats and dire circumstances. Kawerak recommends that if the IAWG is resurrected, and that FEMA could be included to have a key role in the Committee membership. There is a need for the State and Federal Government programs to come together, problem solve and involve appropriate tribal entities; we are all serving the same constituents.

The picture above is the beginning of the Shaktoolik coastal berm. Photo: Anna Rose MacArthur (KNOM, July 2014) Photo to the right is an aerial photo of Shaktoolik.

Shaktoolik, Alaska is one of the communities that was reported in the 2009 federal Government Accountability Office report as ''likely need[ing] to move all at once and as soon as possible.'' The community recognized that funding was extremely limited and decided to take the initiative upon themselves to begin to address their erosion issue. As reported to KNOM radio, in order to possibly prevent significant damage to infrastructure, and the community and to protect safety and life to residents, the City of Shaktoolik after two years of pooling grant funds from the local Community Development Quota (CDQ) group($620,000), with modified plans from the Department of Transportation, began construction this summer of a driftwood pile, embedded with gravel and backed by a gravel mound. If the berm is properly engineered and maintained as a protective measure for the community, it can be eligible under the FEMA public assistance program if damaged in future storms.

Seawalls are needed, but nearly impossible to obtain due to the cost. The below photos come from Teller, Alaska.

The picture above is the beginning of the Shaktoolik coastal berm. Photo: Anna Rose MacArthur (KNOM, July 2014) Photo to the right is an aerial photo of Shaktoolik.

Teller was informed that there could be no repairs to a seawall built in the 1960s. Over the years, more of the shore has eroded, and water damage to the electrical lines of the fuel tanks occurred and the sewage lagoon behind the school was flooded. A seawall could have prevented this from occurring.

After last year's fall storm, Kawerak began efforts to prepare our regional communities to be better prepared for future disasters. An Emergency Management Seminar was held last April, 2014 in Anchorage, Alaska with another one planned for the fall of 2014. This joint seminar sponsored by the Alaska Federation of Natives' Council for Advancement of Alaska Natives, of which our Kawerak President is the Chairperson, the State of Alaska and FEMA participated, is an example of what can work well when key stakeholders jointly work towards solutions. The session focused on best practices, resources available and identified gaps in the disaster process. The group of residents who attended from the regions of Bering Strait, Tanana Chief's Conference and the Association of Village Council Presidents identified the following gaps in disaster preparedness:

- Help more communities develop Small Community Emergency Response Plans (deals with the first 72 hours of a disaster) and Emergency Operation Plans (more long term). Currently, the Alaska Native Tribal Health Consortium has two staff assisting tribal communities with Emergency Operations Plans (EOP), and the State of Alaska works with local municipalities to assist them as well. However, funding is again limited. Establishing an EOP requires professional services, and there are some rural communities who do not even have a municipal government, thus have very little recognition or support from the State of Alaska. Technical assistance and training is needed to be made available through federal and state departments of Homeland Security (in a coordinated manner) and through FEMA.
  Should a tribe seek a disaster declaration directly, having separate tribal plans is redundant in a small community where it is often difficult for a city office to develop a Community Emergency Response Plan or a Hazard Mitigation Plan. Kawerak recommends FEMA allow a tribe to utilize a city plan (if they have one) and/or adopt a city plan as their own in order to meet this requirement.

- Tribes are not able to meet the 25 percent cost share match if they make disaster declarations requests. Although tribes can declare a disaster directly to FEMA the non-federal cost share is an issue. The Bering Strait region tribes do not have available savings or do not have industry services such as gaming or mineral resources to generate revenue to meet the required financial cost-share-match. When the State of Alaska declares a disaster and FEMA funds relief efforts, 75 percent is covered by the Federal Government and 25 percent by the State. So from Kawerak's viewpoint, it's actually a detriment to the tribe if they by-pass the state and declare a disaster directly to FEMA. Resources to carry out projects in our region have been very limited and often funding opportunities require a cost-benefit analysis that factors in population or require a local cost-share that is prohibitive.

- For example, The USACE cost share for projects is prohibitive. Shishmaref has a revetment project to protect their sewage lagoon and washeteria, and it has been on hold because the tribe needs to come up with an $8 million dollar match. For the Elim harbor the cost-benefit analysis proved not to pan-out because it didn't create new jobs with a new harbor. If a cost-share structure is necessary, there should be consideration for cost-sharing between the Federal Government and the state government. Tribal governments in Alaska have practically no tax base to afford a cost share.
- Red tape that is prohibitive to accessing funds should be identified. A national call to tribes and rural communities to identify barriers should be undertaken. For Alaska, the regional non-profits could coordinate obtaining this information.
- Small communities lack adequate emergency responders and equipment, and the limited responders may experience stress in a disaster as well (they may have personal loses themselves).
- If communication systems go down in an emergency, few communities have a backup communication system and are therefore cut off from communication. Stebbins experienced a loss or spotty communication during the storm. Satellite emergency phones should be made available to all high risk communities.
- Small communities need access to training and technical assistance for disaster planning and drills.
- Very few communities have up to date alarm systems or adequate disaster supplies and equipment (generators).
- More rural grant writers are needed to access mitigation funding for emergency preparedness.
- Land ownership and legal address problems keep people from getting reimbursement for disaster losses.
- Federal and state agency staff land on the ground in an emergency, while locals are still stabilizing the community. They often need housing when there is limited housing for evacuees, and need to talk to the people who are the first responders when they need to be out working. [Kawerak proposes FEMA travel to the site earlier. Since there seems to be differing opinions, FEMA should ask the community to determine what is the best time to travel to the impacted community.]

What seemed to resonate, as I prepared this testimony, was the lack of communication between FEMA and stakeholders. The following recommendations may help improve this:

- Develop a preparedness outreach campaign to educate and inform rural communities on concrete steps they can take to increase their resilience to natural and man-made hazards.
- Improve training and technical assistance opportunities for all rural communities. Allow regional support entities like Kawerak, Inc. to be eligible to apply for funding to provide this kind of support to the tribes that they serve through the establishment of full-time staff positions, specializing in disaster risk reduction and emergency management. Storms and disasters do not typically only affect one community—in most cases an entire region is affected. Regional plans are needed and the regional non-profits could provide a mechanism to accomplish this, especially in areas where there are no organized boroughs.
- Improve training opportunities in rural Alaska for all emergency preparedness issues, as well as the declaration process and the programs available. Provide travel scholarships so more rural leaders can attend trainings. Provide more village-based training to enable communities to effectively drill and practice emergency plans.
- Use local resources in planning response efforts. The networking of local knowledge holders with those who have the technical knowledge is needed. Local, Regional, Tribal, State and Federal partnerships when disasters occur is needed. If a spill or an incident were to occur in our backyard, our tribal members will not stand by. Our pristine environment and the sea mammals, birds, fish and land animals are at stake. We have Traditional Ecological Knowledge that is valuable in any planning and response effort.

On July 16, 2014 an oil spill response drill was held in Teller, Alaska. The goal was to determine degree of readiness and to test the logistics of getting oil spill response equipment from Nome to Teller. The Tribal Council President Wesley Okbaok was present and was able to assist the response crew with information about the currents and their behavior in certain wind conditions, as reported in the Nome Nugget Newspaper (July 24, 2014 issue). Cheryl Fultz, environmental compliance specialist with Delta Western, who was present at the drill, stated she learned the most from Wesley. "When you meet a gentleman like Wesley, you realize all of the talent available in the region. The community lives off the sea, and to that end they know every nuance of how the waters behave."
Within the Bering Strait region, another group called the Bering Sea Alliance (comprised of several communities) formed to address the impacts of increased shipping. This proactive group is working with Shell Oil Company to address issues related to disaster prevention and response.

- Although the State of Alaska developed a Small Community Emergency Response Plan (SCERP) template which provides guidance and assistance to any community that wishes to develop such a plan and it provides valuable information on what to do in the first 72 hours after a disaster, education on disaster assistance processes for communities which have been impacted by disasters is needed. Many of our communities didn't know who to contact or how the process works; those villages more familiar with disasters seem to navigate through the process easier.
For example, although a disaster declaration was issued for the November 2013 storm, Elim, Alaska did not seek assistance for damage due to the storm to one of their roads. Elim spent a little over $5,000 dollars clearing driftwood and other debris from Moses Point using BIA Road Maintenance funds (Elim receives $42,600 a year in BIA Road Maintenance funds). Elim did not fix the road to its original specs; but removed the debris to make the road passable. Dirt was added to the four mile damaged stretch, of the nine mile road and added an eight foot sand berm on the most vulnerable areas of the road so far this summer. Elim anticipates expending all or more of their BIA Road Maintenance funds to make the road safe and usable. Elim secured an additional $73,000 from a commercial fish company to reinforce the road infrastructure at the end of the Moses Pt road where boats are parked. Had Elim been aware that they could seek disaster assistance, Elim could possibly have leveraged their roads maintenance funds (and the funds from the commercial fishing company) to help meet match requirements. Therefore, using limited tribal roads maintenance funds in other needed areas.
Another example is with the Stebbins disaster. The Tribal President still doesn't know who the right person is with FEMA to communicate with/to. He didn't know the tribe could seek reimbursement for the expenses they incurred when helping disaster victims after the storm. He heard about the potential to seek reimbursement from a local resident of Nome; not from FEMA personnel. FEMA may be communicating with the City of Stebbins office, but per the Tribal Council President, communication is not occurring with him.
Back in August of 2013, Gambell and Savoonga on St. Lawrence Island received an Economic Disaster Declaration from the Governor of Alaska. For six months, the State of Alaska Department of Commerce, Community and Economic Development coordinated and hosted regular teleconferences with both community leadership (city and tribal offices), and agencies who may be able to assist in some way. The calls started out on a weekly basis, then moved to bi-weekly and near the end, on a monthly basis. This was very helpful; FEMA should consider this when a disaster occurs.

- Establish further collaboration with rural communities, tribes and rural resources available. The U.S.C.G. has actively established relationships with, communicated with, and coordinated with tribes in our region. Other agencies such as FEMA, USACOE and the Department of Homeland Security (both state and federal) should follow suit.

The Bering Strait is the gateway in and out of the Arctic Ocean for migrating marine mammals and seabirds. The Bering Strait is also a gateway for maritime transportation. Vessels traveling from the Pacific to the Arctic—or transiting the Arctic using the Northern Sea Route or Northwest Passage—have no choice but to pass through the bottleneck of the Bering Strait. Our life highly revolves around subsistence activities and the marine environment. Increased ship traffic has the potential to significantly impact the marine life/environment and our subsistence way of life. There is a history (1989 Exxon Valdez oil spill, in 2004 Selendang Ayu oil spill went aground and resulted in the a spill of approximately 336,000 gallons of fuel oil and diesel fuel) that shows that manmade disasters are sure to occur. The question is not if they will occur, it is when, and are we able to respond to the disasters in a timely fashion.

This is a major concern for the people of the Bering Strait region. At recent food security workshops held by the Alaska Inuit Circumpolar Conference, it was reported that from an Inuit perspective, a threat to food security threatens an entire cultural way of life. The Exxon Valdez spilled 11 million gallons of crude oil, and the coastal ecosystem injured by the Exxon Valdez spill is still a long way from full recovery. Therefore, a potential spill would have long term social and cultural impacts to the way of life of residents in the Bering Strait region. Its impacts would also be felt by other Alaskan communities outside the region who rely on the animals which migrate through the strait.

The closest U.S. Coast Guard base is in Kodiak, Alaska and that is over 1,000 miles away. It would take over one day of ocean travel by a Cutter, 2 hours by C–130 and 5 hours by HM–60 helicopter. Response agencies such as FEMA, and the Alaska Red Cross are located in Anchorage, Alaska. There is a huge gap in adequate response time for the Northern Bering Sea and Norton and Kotzebue Sound waters. Response to a disaster will not be immediate, it may take hours and it may even take days depending on the weather.

Up until just a few years ago, the USCG had a Loran Station at Port Clarence in the Bering Strait Region. This station has been shuttered and our region's nearest station is now Kodiak, much too far away. Given the recent increase in ocean vessel traffic through the Bering Strait, increased presence is needed. A permanent USCG base in the Bering Strait, the chokepoint between Russia and Alaska, is needed.

Normal spring hunting conditions include access to open water, availability to secure floating ice, and safe wind directions. In May 2013, unfavorable northerly winds and high ice concentrations along the northern coastlines of Gambell and Savoonga greatly limited access to walrus as they passed through during the spring migration period. The combination of weather factors reduced the number of days during which subsistence hunters would actually be able to access walrus which were located deeper beyond the large ice floes near the communities resulting in a poor walrus harvest. Pacific Walrus is the main food consumed by residents at approximately 120 lbs. each month. It is critical for the continued cultural, nutritional, economic, spiritual well-being, and food security for the residents. The 10-year (2003–2012) average spring walrus harvest for Gambell and Savoonga for the months of March -June is 978 (uncorrected factor). The Native Village of Savoonga and Gambell reported a substantially lower walrus harvest of 180 during the May 2013 subsistence hunting season. Residents rely on the available marine resources as a food source and the lack of a normal walrus harvest has significant economic impacts that prevent additional financial resources from the sale of ivory. The lack of these resources impacts the ability to purchase gas or ammunition to hunt for other available food sources such as seals or birds. Spring 2014 harvest numbers are again lower than normal, and the communities are again bracing for another disaster due to a shortage of food in the community caused by unique weather conditions that impacts hunting. Although the disaster that Gambell and Savoonga experienced was not due to flooding, earthquake or typhoon, the shortage of food created by their natural environment contributed to a dire situation. A response to unique disaster situation such as this, need to be made available.

In conclusion, The Stafford Act is a response when a disaster happens, which is important. But, due to changing climate conditions, changing sea ice conditions and melting permafrost and the extreme variations in the weather, our communities are in imminent danger and preventative measures are needed. No person, in the most developed country in the world, should be subject to the threat of loss of life due to conditions that can be mitigated by governmental actions. The United States provides humanitarian efforts to other countries; often times spending millions of dollars in aid. Our local populations may be small; but we are impacted just the same when disasters occur. We still deserve support and relief, similar to when disaster assistance and support is mobilized to other countries around the world or to lower 48 coastal communities. The U.S. is an arctic nation and has an obligation to assert its sovereign authority and protect national interests. With the authority comes responsibility for disaster prevention, mitigation, and response, especially in an area such as the Bering Strait Region, which is extremely remote and exposed to international ocean traffic.

Thank you for providing time to testify on this important issue.

Additional Storm Photos:

Additional Storm Photos:

2011 storm photos
Little Diomede:

Golovin:

St. Michael (photo by Charlene Austin):

Shaktoolik (photo by Elmer Bekoalok):

2012 Nome storm photo:

The CHAIRMAN. Mary, thank you for making the trek to Washington, D.C. We appreciate your testimony.

Jake Heflin, you are up.

### STATEMENT OF JAKE HEFLIN, PRESIDENT/CEO, TRIBAL EMERGENCY MANAGEMENT ASSOCIATION

Mr. HEFLIN. Chairman Tester, members of the Committee, my name is Jake Heflin. I am the President and Chief Executive Officer for the Tribal Emergency Management Association, or iTEMA. I am an enrolled citizen of the Osage Nation, or Wah Zha Zhi Nation, out of Oklahoma.

On behalf of iTEMA, I want to thank for you holding a hearing on When Catastrophe Strikes: Responses to Natural Disasters in Indian Country. With over 23 years of experience in emergency services, I have served in various capacities to include firefighter, paramedic and community emergency response team, or CERT program manager. I currently work for the City of Long Beach Fire Department in California.

iTEMA is a national tribal organization comprised of volunteers that focus on tribal emergency management and emergency services. The mission of iTEMA is to promote a collaborative, multi-disciplinary approach to coordinate and enhance emergency management, response and recovery to protect all tribal communities.

As an emergency responder and emergency management instructor that works with tribal governments throughout Indian Country, it has become evident that there is a significant disparity between the state of readiness for tribal communities versus that of local, county and State governments. It boils down to capacity, capability, and funding. With an increasing number of challenging and escalating incidents impacting Indian Country, it is apparent that a solution is necessary to address this disparity. Identifying ways for impacted tribes to request assistance from tribes and/or other Federal partners or tribal emergency management experts and organizations like iTEMA during an emergency incident is critical.

When a catastrophe strikes, the Federal response to natural disasters in Indian Country is slow, tedious and in significant need of a comprehensive overhaul. Coordinated planning and preparedness activities initiated by tribes and the Federal Government are important. These initiatives lessen the impacts of disasters in Indian Country. However, more support is needed.

Despite providing pre-disaster support and technical assistance and planning before disaster strikes, at the time of the incident FEMA is not really available until monetary thresholds are met by the disaster. Even when FEMA responds to disaster, FEMA does not support the tribes operationally.

iTEMA believes that as an association we should be utilized and provided with the opportunity to support the Bureau of Indian Affairs and support FEMA through development of memorandums of understanding to support our direct participation and response. iTEMA recommends that Federal funding be set aside to further support the continued development and maintenance of the Tribal Emergency Mutual Aid Compact, or TEMAC. Given the specific complexities associated with emergency response in Indian Country, iTEMA believes that there should be a specific tribal emergency support function, or tribal ESF, within the national response framework. A tribal ESF would further enhance the visibility of tribes at the Federal level. The Tribal Assistance Coordination Group, or TAC–G, is an example of the successful strategy in increased communications with tribes and other Federal partners.

Additional work must be done to meet the needs of tribal communities. The development of tribal CERT programs, tribal fire and EMS programs and tribal emergency management programs should be supported nationally through direct funding to tribes. This program must be funded to meet the current demand and open to all tribes that show a need and can articulate a plan for developing these services.

iTEMA asks that the Congressional Research Services investigate the state of tribal emergency management and emergency services, as there is inconsistent information as to the state of readiness in Indian Country. The current capacity and capabilities

51

of tribal emergency services are, for the most part, relatively un-known. An assessment and clearinghouse for this information should be established.

The Federal Government plays a pivotal role in Indian Country during emergencies. They have the ability to bring robust capability of supplemental disaster funding to support tribes. The reality is, though, that within Indian Country, most incidents will never meet the Federal Government thresholds and the available Federal support will be minimal. This must change.

The thresholds of presidentially-declared disasters must be looked at from a tribal perspective, not a hard number. Tribes are different. Incidents impacting our sacred sites don't carry monetary value. For us, it is priceless, our people, our culture, our ways of life, those are our most precious resources.

I ask today that Congress fund the Federal Government to establish a baseline for tribal emergency response and recovery. I ask that the Federal Government look to their tribal partners to find solutions that empower Indian Country to be self-reliant. This requires funding and an overhaul of the current system.

Emergency management funding must be provided directly to the tribes. Access to these funds is necessary in order to support the development of tribal capacity and capability. To minimize loss, we must take a proactive approach in dealing with natural catastrophes. We must focus on preparedness and mitigation to reduce the loss associated with response and recovery.

In conclusion, I appreciate the opportunity to speak today. I look forward to working together to promote and enhance emergency management response and recovery throughout Indian Country. Thank you, and I am open to any questions you might have, sir.

[The prepared statement of Mr. Heflin follows:]

PREPARED STATEMENT OF JAKE HEFLIN, PRESIDENT/CEO, TRIBAL EMERGENCY MANAGEMENT ASSOCIATION

Chairman Tester, Vice Chairman Barrasso and Members of the Committee, my name is Jake Heflin, I am the President and Chief Executive Officer for the Tribal Emergency Management Association, also known as iTEMA. I am an enrolled Citizen of the Wah Zha Zhi Nation (Osage Nation) out of Oklahoma. I am from the Tzi-Zho Wah-Shtah-Keh Clan. I was given the name Tah-Wah Gka-Keh ''Town Maker''.

On behalf of iTEMA, I want to thank for you holding a hearing on ''When Catastrophe Strikes: Responses to Natural Disasters in Indian Country.''

With over 23 years of experience in emergency services, I have served as a Firefighter, Paramedic, Field Supervisor, Field Training Officer, Paramedic Preceptor and Community Emergency Response Team (CERT) Program Manager. I currently work for the City of Long Beach Fire Department in California.

iTEMA is a national tribal organization comprised of volunteers that focus on Tribal Emergency Management and Emergency Services. The mission of iTEMA is to promote a collaborative, multi-disciplinary approach to prepare for, protect against, respond to, recover from, and mitigate against all hazards that impact our Tribal communities.

As an emergency responder and emergency management instructor that works with Tribal governments throughout Indian Country, it has become evident that there is a significant disparity between the state of readiness for Tribal communities versus that of local, county, and State government. It boils down to capacity, capability, and funding.

With an increasing number of challenging and escalating incidents impacting Indian Country, it is apparent that a solution is necessary to address this disparity. Identifying ways for impacted Tribes to request assistance from other Tribes and/or other federal and Tribal emergency management experts like iTEMA during an emergency incident is critical. Immediate emergency operational assistance, whether it is simply to provide support over the phone or actually deploy resources, is, for the most part, an unmet need for Indian Country. Tribes are left to fend for themselves, with minimal assistance and cooperation from local and State agencies. These reoccurring events led to the creation of iTEMA.

iTEMA strives to provide technical assistance that supports Tribes as they prepare and consider critical information for declaring a State of Emergency, tracking costs associated with the event, managing resources and the corresponding documentation that supports requests for reimbursement should the event meet the thresholds for a Presidential Declaration.

iTEMA also provides training opportunities by way of our annual conference and we offer specific classes targeted at increasing emergency capacity and capabilities. iTEMA assists in development of Tribal CERT programs and developing comprehensive plans that help Tribal communities take proactive steps to minimize and mitigate loss associated with future events. Efforts are currently underway by iTEMA, individual Tribes, and other partners such as the State of California Office of Emergency Services to develop Tribal Incident Management Teams to further provide additional resources for Tribal communities.

When a catastrophe strikes, the Federal response to natural disasters in Indian Country is slow, tedious and in significant need of a comprehensive overhaul. Coordinated planning and preparedness activities initiated by Tribes and the Federal Government are important. These initiatives lessen the impacts of disasters in Indian Country. However, more support is needed. The United States Federal Government has taken some small steps to enhance the outreach and opportunities to support these initiatives, but lacks the operational coordination when working with Tribes on real events. For example, despite providing pre-disaster support, technical assistance and planning before a disaster strikes, at the time of the incident, FEMA steps away from Tribes until monetary thresholds are met by the disaster. Even when FEMA responds to a disaster, FEMA does not support the Tribes operationally.

Currently, the systems that are in place to support Indian Country during disasters rely heavily on the Federal Government to provide All Hazards Emergency Response Operations (A–HERO) support during events that impact Tribes. Often, this assistance from the Federal Government is provided by part-time or on call staffing that have no specific experience relating to the emergency needs of Tribal communities.

Tribes are uniquely different. As sovereigns, Tribes have a responsibility to provide for the public safety of their citizens. However, when Tribes are overwhelmed by a disaster, the Federal Government has a trust responsibility to support Tribes and provide the appropriate assistance.

The current National Response Framework does not adequately identify a primary Federal lead for disasters in Indian Country. However, iTEMA believes that the response model for Indian Country needs to include FEMA, the Bureau of Indian Affairs, other Federal Partners and non-governmental organizations like iTEMA for increased support and involvement.

During disasters, first responders play a pivotal role in a Tribe's ability to manage the incident. In the areas of Tribal Structural Fire and Tribal Emergency Medical Services, there is minimal federal engagement to support these programs. Wildland Fire responsibilities in Indian Country already exist under the Bureau of Indian Affairs. Thus, iTEMA proposes bringing these additional emergency services together under the Bureau of Indian Affairs Emergency Management division to create a comprehensive all-hazard, all-risk approach to managing response throughout Indian Country.

iTEMA believes that as an association, with a focus on Tribal emergency response, we should be utilized and provided with the opportunity to support the Bureau of Indian Affairs and FEMA, through the development of a Memorandum of Understanding to support our direct participation in response. The Tribes would see a marked change in the level of experience and awareness that these responders bring to Tribal communities in need of support and assistance.

iTEMA recommends that Federal funding be set aside to further support the continued development and maintenance of a Tribal Emergency Mutual Aid Compact (TEMAC). Just as the National Emergency Management Association receives funding to support the State to State mutual aid (EMAC), iTEMA believes we are well positioned to manage this effort on behalf of Indian Country. This process will support Tribes in a more effective manner and streamline the process for Tribes to receive outside support from other Tribes and Tribal organizations.

Given the specific complexities associated with emergency response in Indian Country, iTEMA believes that there should be a specific Tribal Emergency Support

Function (ESF) within the National Response Framework (NRF). ESF's provide structure for coordinating Federal interagency support as it relates the how the Federal Government responds to an incident. A Tribal ESF would further enhance the visibility of Tribes at the Federal level with regard to response. The Tribal Assistance Coordination Group (TAC–G) is an example of a successful strategy to increase communications with Tribes and other Federal partners.

Additional work must be done to meet the needs of Tribal communities. The development of Tribal CERT, Tribal Fire and EMS programs and Tribal Emergency Management programs should be supported nationally through direct funding to the Tribes. This program must be funded to meet the current demand and opened to all Tribes that show a need and can articulate a plan for developing these services.

The Tribal Coordination Support Annex, part of the National Response Framework, should be released immediately. This annex has already been created but remains tangled in red tape and bureaucracy for unknown reasons.

iTEMA asks that Congressional Research Services investigate the state of Tribal emergency management and emergency services as there is inconsistent information as to the state of readiness in Indian Country. The current capacities and capabilities of Tribal Emergency Services are, for the most part, not really known. An assessment and a clearinghouse for this important information must be established, in order for Tribes to share this important information between agencies and other partners. Indian Country must have better snapshot of our current state of Tribal Emergency Services to better identify the unmet needs that exist.

The strategic, operational, and tactical aspects of Tribal emergencies from the United States Federal Government must be handled by those with the background and experience to do so. Currently, FEMA, at the Headquarters level, chooses to house Tribal Affairs in FEMA Intergovernmental Affairs, part of FEMA External Affairs. Despite recommendations from Indian Country and other Federal Government partners, FEMA Headquarters has not realized the importance of placing Tribal All Hazards Emergency Response Operations (A–HERO) within the FEMA Office of Response and Recovery. Even at the FEMA regional level, some FEMA Regional Directors have chosen to move Tribal emergency operations out of External Affairs, into more appropriate places, like the FEMA Regional Preparedness Branch.

The Federal Government plays a pivotal role in Indian Country during emergencies. They have the ability to bring robust capability and supplemental disaster funding to support Tribes. The reality is that within Indian Country, most incidents will never meet the Federal Government thresholds and the available Federal support will be minimal. This must change. The thresholds of Presidentially Declared Disasters must be looked at from a Tribal perspective, not a hard number. Tribes are different. Incidents impacting our sacred sites don't carry a monetary value. For us, it's priceless. Our people, our culture, our way of life are our most valuable resources. For Tribes, emergency management is something we have practiced for centuries. However, with a changing climate and escalating technological hazards, Tribes are at increased risk.

I ask today, that Congress fund the Federal Government to establish a baseline for Tribal emergency response and recovery. I ask that the Federal Government look to their Tribal partners to find solutions that empower Indian County to be self-reliant. This requires funding and an overhaul of the current system. Emergency Management funding must be provided directly to Tribes. Access to these funds is necessary in order to support the development of Tribal capacity and capability. To minimize loss, we must take a proactive approach when dealing with natural catastrophes. We must focus on preparedness and mitigation to reduce the loss associated with response and recovery.

iTEMA is an organization that was created to support Tribes during disasters. It was built on the premise of "Tribes helping Tribes". iTEMA is committed to working with the Federal Government to develop and implement these solutions.

In conclusion, I sincerely appreciate the opportunity to speak today and look forward to working together to promote and enhance emergency management, response, and recovery throughout Indian Country.

Thank you and I am open to any questions you may have.

The CHAIRMAN. Jake, thank you for your testimony. I thank all the participants on this panel for their testimony.

Senator Begich?

Senator BEGICH. Thank you very much, Mr. Chairman.

Mary, thank you for coming. I know the trip is long and I appreciate you being here. Thank you for your testimony and thank you for the work you do with Kawerak and many of the tribes there.

I have a few questions for you. You talked about the storm in November 2013 in the Bering Straits and the region. Can you provide some examples of work being done in the villages to kind of better prepare for future disasters? Along with that, can you add how has FEMA worked with you or not with this new tribal office?

Ms. DAVID. It has been a slow process. I think when the Immediate Action Work Group work ended back in 2011, I think it got even slower. Kawerak recognized that every year we continually have fall and early winter storms. To be proactive, the State of Alaska has a spring preparedness conference. Before that conference began this year, the AFN Council for Advancement of Native Americans had a pre-session. That was beneficial for the representatives from Kawerak, ABCPNTCC. So that type of activity occurred, and another one is planned for this fall before AFN begins.

Senator BEGICH. Was FEMA a part of that?

Ms. DAVID. Yes.

Senator BEGICH. The State and FEMA and other agencies?

Ms. DAVID. And other agencies, yes.

Senator BEGICH. Very good. So you found that beneficial?

Ms. DAVID. Yes.

Senator BEGICH. And do you know of other trainings or activity that you all, from your region or any other region you might know of, that utilizes FEMA training?

Ms. DAVID. No.

Senator BEGICH. Is there a way that maybe, sometimes communicating or getting information out, especially in Alaska, especially rural Alaska, is not as simple as just running a TV ad, but are there ways you would recommend for FEMA, especially with their new tribal office, to be very proactive in getting information out on these training opportunities? For example, there was a mention when I was asking the last speaker, in regard to how many people participated in FEMA training from tribal communities, there was a sizeable amount. But are there suggestions you might have on what we could do or we could suggest to FEMA on how to communicate to tribes on what is available in FEMA for specialized training around emergency preparedness and other needs?

Ms. DAVID. I think it is challenging in rural Alaska, because internet connection is very slow. So I think the best possible way to communicate is probably through each non-profit regional corporation. In our region, each region has a tribal coordinator that we employ. So for us in our region, communication through Kawerak, through our tribal coordinator who works, who is the office support for the tribe, would probably be the best way.

Senator BEGICH. Do the tribal coordinators get together on a regular basis from the other tribes at all, in any kind of conference or activity like that? I am just trying to ask you this, through you to the administrator behind you. I am trying to give her some ideas.

Ms. DAVID. I think most attend the BIA conference in Anchorage.

Senator BEGICH. So the BIA conference might be a great avenue for the tribal coordinators?

Ms. DAVID. Yes.

Senator BEGICH. You mentioned the Immediate Action Work Group. Can you tell me the status of where that is at, active, not active?

Ms. DAVID. It is not active at this time.

Senator BEGICH. Who instigates, who would instigate getting that back into activity?

Ms. DAVID. I believe it would be the governor of Alaska.

Senator BEGICH. Do you think FEMA might have a role to help initiate that?

Ms. DAVID. Yes, I do. They would play, I believe, an important role in that, with that group.

Senator BEGICH. And the Immediate Action Work Group you found to be beneficial?

Ms. DAVID. Yes.

Senator BEGICH. Because it created communication, right?

Ms. DAVID. It was.

Senator BEGICH. So maybe that is something we could work with FEMA on, if the governor is unwilling to do it, maybe FEMA might be able to initiate that working group, because the value you found for not only your region, but all regions was of high value.

Ms. DAVID. Yes, it was. If I could add a comment?

Senator BEGICH. Yes, absolutely.

Ms. DAVID. So the Immediate Action Work Group was actually formed under Governor Palin. She established a climate change sub-cabinet and then the Immediate Action Work Group was comprised of Federal, State and local officials to come up with ways to protect Alaska's most at-risk communities.

Senator BEGICH. So that was a sub-group underneath the cabinet group?

Ms. DAVID. Yes.

Senator BEGICH. Okay. Because I know the governor has eliminated that sub-cabinet meeting on climate change, so therefore eliminated that, that working group.

Ms. DAVID. I believe so.

Senator BEGICH. So maybe we could work with you and maybe FEMA, and again, I am kind of talking through you to make sure FEMA is hearing what I am saying. She is nodding behind you, which is a good sign. So maybe that is an opportunity we could work on, to have better communication on this.

Mr. Chairman, the only thing I will add is, I heard a couple of times, and I know Mr. Gregory brought it up also, and others did, on this threshold of a million dollars. I am assuming that has been triggering your mind, too, as something of interest of how we make sure we can accommodate potentially that issue. It sounds like rural areas, and you asked that question earlier about what is causing the problem. Well, this may be one of the problems. The number is too large and we have, in a small village in Alaska, I can tell you half a million dollars would be devastating. Yet we wouldn't reach the million dollar threshold, so we are kind of in this quandary. So it was really more of a rhetorical question.

Thank you, Mary, for being here, and thank you for the travel.

The CHAIRMAN. Thank you, Senator Begich.

You are right, that is exactly the line of questioning I was going to go down right off the bat, since we had the Governor mention it, and again Matt Gregory mentioned it, and others too. I will start with you, Matt. I know FEMA makes the declaration. The question comes from a couple of different perspectives. You talked about how the infrastructure simply wasn't there to reach the million dollar threshold. That is a problem from your perspective, it is not that they are lowballing the amount of damages done, it is just that the infrastructure is not there?

Mr. GREGORY. That is correct. In rural communities, a lot of the State and counties meet that threshold through the infrastructure that they have. So the roads, the utilities and those things. For a tribe in Oklahoma, our situations is very difficult to reach that million dollar threshold.

The CHAIRMAN. So let me ask you this, just to flesh this out a little bit more. You have roads on tribal land, too. Do they count toward the threshold? Like a paved road. Now, I will admit, oftentimes they are not up to the standard outside reservation roads are, and we are going to work on that. But the question comes, they are still eligible, right?

Mr. GREGORY. Because we are in a checkerboard situation, a lot of those are county and city roads. So there is not infrastructure of tribal roads specifically.

The CHAIRMAN. Okay. That is good to know. And as far as utilities, if they are owned by the local co-op they can't count toward your disaster declaration?

Mr. GREGORY. That is correct.

The CHAIRMAN. Thank you.

Governor Chavarria, Santa Clara has had its share of disasters, it would be fair to say, more than its share of interactions with FEMA and other Federal agencies, too, that respond to disasters. You suffered four major wildland fires, correct me if I am wrong.

Governor CHAVARRIA. That is correct.

The CHAIRMAN. The Las Conchas Fire burned over 50 percent of your watershed.

Governor CHAVARRIA. That is correct.

The CHAIRMAN. And that resulted in severe flooding. You made some recommendations based on what you have been through. What is your highest priority for changes that would make the Federal Government work better in protecting lives and property for your people?

Governor CHAVARRIA. It would be to quickly obligate those dollars.

The CHAIRMAN. By that you mean the money for funding?

Governor CHAVARRIA. Project worksheets that identify the direct disaster. We are already a year, almost a year into it, and we still haven't got the majority of our funds for larger projects, because it has to go through a quality assurance, quality control process before those funds are actually obligated or bundled through this system, then we can start to utilize those dollars. That is the quick need for us in Santa Clara, to really get that dollar tomorrow and not wait until the following year.

The CHAIRMAN. I believe this past April you testified in front of the House Appropriations Interior Subcommittee that the Army Corps is recommending construction of a dam within the canyon, correct?

Governor CHAVARRIA. That was at that time, but it is no longer feasible.

The CHAIRMAN. Why is that?

Governor CHAVARRIA. Because they couldn't find a solid foundation to anchor all that foundation. They did some drilling and they couldn't find bedrock.

The CHAIRMAN. So that is off the table but it still remains a problem?

Governor CHAVARRIA. It is off the table. They admitted that the flooding still exists, but they used advanced measures program to now look at temporary types of measures for gabling check structures. Also dredging the channel within the community to give it capacity and also do some Hesco baskets along some earthen berms, and then armoring those earthen berms.

So being that we didn't get the larger $40 million dam project which is more of a permanent type of structure, we have now looked into temporary type measures. The kicker there is on a permanent, we would have had a 25 percent cost match. On these temporary measures, it is being fully absorbed through the Corps of Engineers advanced measures program.

The CHAIRMAN. Okay. Ms. Metcalf, thank you for being here. I appreciate your testimony.

It was brought up earlier by Senator Cantwell about the 19 days that it took for FEMA to make a declaration of an emergency. Do you have an explanation for that delay?

Ms. METCALF. What we were told, why they wouldn't accept the declarations we would send in, is the terminology didn't fit for requesting an emergency declaration.

The CHAIRMAN. Did they say how the terminology didn't fit?

Ms. METCALF. No. It was just change it to this, change it to that. I think one of the biggest problems is the lack of coordination. There were so many people talking, there were so many different people showing up, all from FEMA.

The CHAIRMAN. So there wasn't a point person for FEMA? Or there wasn't a point person from the tribe?

Ms. METCALF. The point person from the tribe was the chairman.

The CHAIRMAN. So there wasn't a point person from FEMA?

Ms. METCALF. No. Different people came all the time.

The CHAIRMAN. Okay. You also in your testimony talked about gas cards that were provided to residents of Darrington but not to tribal members.

Ms. METCALF. Yes.

The CHAIRMAN. Why is that?

Ms. METCALF. We are really not sure. When our tribal members would go stand in line, they would wait two hours in line like everybody else for gas cards, and they were told that they didn't fit the criteria for the gas cards.

The CHAIRMAN. And that was it?

Ms. METCALF. That is all we were told.

The CHAIRMAN. Okay. You talked about the checkerboard, Mr. Gregory, as far as the declaration goes. I want to go a different way with it. Your checkerboard landscape means that there is a lot of non-Indian local government that you have to interact with. How do you do that? What is your best way of interacting with basically non-Indian local governments?

Mr. GREGORY. I think we do that in several ways. We do that by attending the county meetings, the city meetings, working with the emergency managers for the ten and a half county area. We also do planning, we do disaster planning, we invite them to be part of our planning, our tabletops that we have done. We have invited the community out to do those planning sessions with us.

But it also is about, we are community. And the city and the towns and the county governments are all part of our family, we consider. So we work directly with those. We also are part of the State, Oklahoma State Department of Emergency Management.

The CHAIRMAN. So you are fully integrated into all the non-Indian entities?

Mr. GREGORY. We are, and we try to do a better job. There is still work to be done there.

The CHAIRMAN. And they into you?

Mr. GREGORY. Yes, for the most part, yes.

The CHAIRMAN. Okay good. That is good.

Mr. Heflin, you mentioned iTEMA's efforts to provide additional resources to tribes. What is first on your agenda in that regard?

Mr. HEFLIN. I think at a certain point, the question is access. We have heard today that there are inconsistencies as far as who to call, how do we get hold of somebody to help. Where do we make that first call, and there is inconsistent support depending upon the person they are talking to.

For us as an organization, we identified that that was a critical need. So we established a toll-free number to push out to Indian Country to help provide that assistance, so there was one number to help call for a national organization to provide some preliminary guidance and discussion and also make the contact to the corresponding Federal agencies that would have involvement in that, with the support of the TAC–G or the Tribal Assistance Coordination Group. For us, that was the solution to that, because there was such an issue with that, we started noticing throughout Indian Country.

The CHAIRMAN. I just want to say, I have more questions that we will get out to you guys. I want to thank you for making the trip. I want to thank you for what you do, each and every one of you. I want to thank Ms. Zimmerman for staying here for the hearing from FEMA to listen to the concerns. I think if there is one thing that this hearing has pointed out to me is that there is plenty of opportunity for improvement here. I think a lot of it has to do with communication. Maybe we have to tweak the million dollar threshold as it applies to Indian Country, because you are right, a lot of Indian Country, that infrastructure isn't there, or maybe we need to figure out how to allow some of the infrastructure we don't count to count.

I don't know the best way to go about it, but I can guarantee you one thing. If we all work together, we will figure it out. FEMA has to be a part of that equation.

So I want to thank all of you again for your testimony. This hearing is going to remain open for two weeks from today for any further comments people want to put in.

With that, the hearing is adjourned. Thank you again.

[Whereupon, at 4:25 p.m., the hearing was adjourned.]

# APPENDIX

Prepared Statement of Hon. Brian Cladoosby, President, National Congress of American Indians

Honorable Chairman Tester, Vice Chairman Barrasso, and members of the Committee, on behalf of the membership of the National Congress of American Indians, the oldest and largest national tribal government advocacy organization in the country, I appreciate your efforts in conducting this oversight hearing. This follow up to the hearing three years ago, titled *Facing Floods and Fires: Emergency Preparedness for Natural Disasters in Native Communities,* is well-timed as much has happened to call attention to the great needs for financial and technical assistance as tribes seek to enhance emergency management capacity.

## Amendments to the Stafford Act

For decades the Federal Emergency Management Agency has been a state-centric organization and changing the course of the overall agency has proved difficult in the last few years but limited progress has been made in improving consultation with tribal governments. On January 29, 2013 President Obama signed the Sand Recovery Improvement Act. I thank the Committee for supporting this monumental legislation to allow tribal nations to directly request disaster assistance for an emergency or disaster from the Federal Government without having to go through another sovereign government. I also thank FEMA Administrator Craig Fugate for his willingness to support and advocate for tribal declaration authority.

FEMA is currently finalizing its proposed Tribal Consultation Policy and seeking comments for the Tribal Declarations Pilot Guidance. Indian Country leaders hope that administrative policy changes will reflect tribal comments. For instance, Committee Members are well aware of the disparate economic and demographic situation throughout Indian Country which makes it extremely difficult for tribal jurisdictions to meet the Stafford Act damages threshold. The result is that tribal governments and citizens in impoverished areas suffer disproportionately as they do not have the financial means to recover from disaster losses. We hope that FEMA will adopt a favorable formula.

## Indian Country Disasters

The recent wildfire at Santa Clara Pueblo, mudslide at Sauk Suiattle, flooding at Quinault, and hurricane damage at Shinnecock, reinforces that fact that tribal communities have differing levels of preparedness and response capability. Emergency situations and disasters in Indian Country require unique types of assistance for response from the Federal Government. Pre-disaster communication and outreach by FEMA headquarters and regional officials with tribal government officials must occur. On the tribal side, if they have not done so, tribal emergency management directors should be identified and communicate with FEMA and other federal emergency management officials.

## FEMA Staffing

At this Committee's last hearing on Indian Country disasters, Administrator Fugate provided testimony that FEMA "hired ten new permanent, full-time employees as Intergovernmental Tribal Affairs Specialists to work out of each of the FEMA Regions" and that "FEMA also hired an attorney within the Agency's Office of Chief Counsel (OCC) who is trained and experienced in Federal Indian Law." While both of these efforts were worthwhile and helped strengthen the federal-tribal government-to-government relationship between the executive and the tribes, it is unclear that the infrastructure Administrator Fugate described in 2011 is still in place.

In some FEMA regions Regional Tribal Liaisons (RTLs) concentrate full-time on tribal issues. In other regions RTLs are said to dedicate half of their time to tribal issues, but it is our understanding that it is a rarity for an RTL to spend 50 percent of their time on tribal issues. We recommend that the Committee request the FEMA

Administrator to provide a detailed staffing and organization plan of tribal affairs personnel and the reporting structure at HQ and FEMA Regions.

In evaluating all aspects of FEMA's Indian Policy efforts it might be useful for the Committee to direct the Government Accountability Office to look at all of FEMA's tribal relations programs for implementation as well as consistency in staffing and productivity.

### Federal Grant Funding

In the *Implementing the Recommendations of the 9/11 Commission Act of 2007* the Congress established eligibility for Indian tribes for homeland security grant funding. While crafting this legislation Congress wanted to ensure that funding was allocated with a risk-assessment methodology. This methodology created two classes of federally recognized Indian tribes, those that are directly eligible for federal funding and those that are not. FEMA recently adopted a Threat and Hazard Risk Identification and Analysis process to apply this risk evaluation so there is no longer a need for two classes of tribes. All tribes should be eligible to apply and their applications should be evaluated on their merit.

Since 2003 Congress has appropriated over $630 million per year for homeland security and emergency management grants and programs to states, locals, non-profits, and even the private sector. A 2011 report showed that up to that time the country has spent over $630 billion SINCE 9–11. During this same timeframe, the best I can tell is that FEMA has allocated less than $40 million to Indian tribes for the same purposes. State Homeland Security grants totaling $355 million were awarded to 56 states and territories in FY 2013, an average of $6.3 million per state. That same year 28 tribes received $10 million for an average of $.35 million per tribe. Inequitable homeland security funding to tribes is shameful and wrong.

Hazard Mitigation Grant Program provides funding for implementing long-term post disaster mitigation measures to reduce loss of life and property in future disasters. The HMGP guidelines were designed for tribes with significant infrastructure and capability. Whether tribes are grantees or sub-grantees, there needs to be flexibility for tribes to utilize HMGP for developing and completing hazard mitigation plans and for purposes beyond the current guidelines, possibly on a case by case, tribe by tribe basis.

FEMA has devolved some of its federal grant responsibility to states and requires tribes to request funding through states which results in increased burdens on tribes to develop capability. There are many federal grant processes, for which tribes are not eligible, that require legislative or administrative fixes. Some states place additional mandates on Indian tribes as a sub-grantee such as HMGP funding. The NCAI urges the Committee to request the Congressional Research Service to review all necessary legislative changes and provide recommendations to remedy situations in which FEMA is devolving its responsibility or where the law does not provide that Indian tribes are eligible applicants.

### Federal Coordinating Officers and Joint Field Offices

FEMA maintains a standing roster, or cadre, of about forty-five Federal Coordinating Officers who have undergone an agency-wide certification program to prepare them for all-hazard events including terrorism and weapons of mass destruction. FCOs must participate in actual disaster response or full-scale exercises as part of the certification program. FCOs are not required to have any familiarity about basic tribal government operations and functions. Only a few FCOs have undergone any type of Indians 101 training, but according to our information, those who have undergone such training have performed well in assisting tribal communities for which they are responsible in disaster situations. This Committee can help by sending a message to FEMA to develop an FCO course in tribal relations that includes interaction with the DHS and DHS–FEMA HQ Tribal Liaisons.

A Joint Field Office is a multiagency center that facilitates incident management during actual or potential situations including incidents that require a coordinated federal response. Only recently have some FCO's invited tribal officials into the unified coordinating JFO structure. Instead of waiting for disaster situations, FCO's should reach out to and actively communicate with tribal officials and automatically include tribal officials in the JFO during a Presidential Disaster Declaration.

### Tribal Cadre of Disaster Assistance Employees

Disaster Assistance Employees (DAE) are temporary FEMA employees who work in a disaster zone that can be deployed from a few weeks to several months depending on the area and gravity of a disaster. Among the duties of DAEs is to contact tribal officials and apprise them of recovery programs and eligibility requirements as well as assist in filling out and submitting required paperwork. Native peoples' cultural and other differences are better understood by another Native person who would be able to better interact and respond to questions coming from or related to tribal community members. Indian Country would benefit greatly if FEMA would institutionalize a formal qualified tribal DAE cadre. The NCAI requests that this committee urge FEMA to establish the tribal DAE cadre.

## FEMA—Emergency Management Institute

The NCAI passed a resolution (#TUL–13–046) following passage of the Stafford Act tribal amendment calling for appropriate consultation, collaboration, and training of tribal leaders and emergency management officials regarding promulgation of the Act, which recognizes tribal sovereignty. FEMA's Emergency Management Institute (EMI), in collaboration with tribal emergency management specialists, has developed courses to assist tribal government officials in emergency management planning. The unique courses contain tribal cultural, governance, and jurisdictional implications. Tribes are in need of experienced tribal emergency managers to assume Stafford Act disaster declaration responsibility. We ask the Committee Members to seek budgetary support of not less than $500,000 annually for onsite and field delivery of greatly needed and cost effective training.

## Other Recommendations

Tribes have not been invited to testify at other congressional committees regarding disasters and emergency preparedness and when FEMA testifies before other committees we do not hear tribal issues being highlighted or even mentioned. We hope members of this Committee will assist in ensuring that tribes will be included in all hearings regarding this important topic.

We urge the Committee to request the Congressional Research Service to report on the possible legislative actions related to tribal emergency management that the Congress should consider. Specifically the CRS should evaluate the Stafford Act and the Sandy Recovery and Improvement Act and recommend changes for tribal participation and consider whether separate tribal disaster laws are needed.

## In Closing

At this 2011 hearing on disasters in Indian Country, Committee Vice Chairman Barrasso stated, "Often we don't pay much attention to the need for emergency preparedness until after there is a disaster, but the risk of one form or another of natural disaster in Indian Country is not theoretical and, as we can see, it is real, and Indian communities need to be prepared to deal with this reality." This statement, unfortunately, is still accurate. The National Congress of American Indians thanks the Committee for looking into this vital topic and for the opportunity to submit our statement. We look to the Committee to lead Indian Country into an enhanced state of emergency preparedness which will benefit citizens of tribal communities as well as our nation as a whole.

————

PREPARED STATEMENT OF HON. JO-ELLEN DARCY, ASSISTANT SECRETARY OF THE ARMY (CIVIL WORKS)

Chairman Tester, Ranking Member Barrasso, and Members of the Committee, I am Jo-Ellen Darcy, Assistant Secretary of the Army (Civil Works). Thank you for the opportunity to provide a Statement for the Record, discussing the Army Corps of Engineers (Corps) response to natural disasters in Indian Country. The Corps prepares for and provides timely, consistent, and efficient execution of response and recovery operations for flood and other natural disasters to save lives, protect property and the environment, and to meet basic human needs. The Corps provides this support to State, Tribes and local governments under Public Law 84–99 and supports FEMA under the Stafford Act, as amended.

Public Law 84–99 authorizes the Chief of Engineers, acting through the Secretary of the Army, to undertake activities including disaster preparedness, Advance Measures, emergency operations (flood response and Post Flood Response), rehabilitation of flood control works threatened by or destroyed by flood, protection or repair of federally authorized shore protective works threatened or damaged by coastal storms, provision of emergency water due to contaminated sources, and drought assistance. With the single exception of drought assistance, which is due to the specific language of the statute, Tribal Nations can, and do, request and receive assistance under PL 84–99 from the Corps.

The Stafford Act (Public Law 93–288, as amended), constitutes the statutory authority for most Federal response activities, especially as they pertain to FEMA and FEMA programs. In accordance with the Stafford Act, FEMA may direct the Corps to utilize its available personnel, supplies, facilities, or other resources to provide assistance in the event of a major disaster or emergency declaration. The Department of Defense has designated the Corps as the planning and operating agent for Emergency Support Function #3, Public Works and Engineering, under FEMA's National Response Framework (NRF). FEMA's NRF provides guidance for the Nation's all-hazards response, and identifies key organizational response principles, roles, and structures.

The Stafford Act was amended in the Sandy Recovery Improvement Act of 2013 (Public Law 113–2), to provide federally recognized tribal governments the choice to request emergency and major disaster declarations. This allows FEMA, and other Federal agencies as directed, to provide assistance to tribal governments independently of state declarations. I'm going to share a few examples of support that the Corps has provided to Tribal Nations in response to natural disasters.

Last April, the Saint Regis Mohawk Tribe was affected by flooding in Franklin and St. Lawrence Counties. A small dam at Saint Regis Falls in Waverly, NY had breached, spilling water onto Tribal lands, inundating roads and requiring the evacuation of 10–12 homes. The Tribe had used all of their available sand bags and was in need of additional sand bags. The Tribe contacted one of the Corps tribal liaisons, and from there the Corps Buffalo District contacted the Tribe. Arrangements were made within the hour for the Tribe to pick up a supply of sandbags at a Corps' storage facility located about 100 miles away.

The Quinault Indian Nation live, hunt, and fish on the same land and waters as their ancestors did centuries ago. Three Indian reservations of the Quinault Indian Nation, the Quinault, Hoh Indian Tribe and Quileute Tribe, are located on the Washington coast. All three villages are located at sea level and at the confluence of major rivers. In the summer of 1993, the Corps Seattle District developed a list of environmental triggers, that when reached, would indicate imminent flooding, thereby threatening historic villages and heavily populated areas occupied by Tribal elders and others who may be reluctant to leave their ancestral homes, even temporarily. When teams for this coastal area conducted exercises in the late summer of 2013 to prepare for flood season, they had these triggers in hand and were able to develop a preferred course of action during a potential flood event. This pre-planning paid off when these triggers were met in January 2014 by a flood event caused by a combination of high tides, high winds, storm surges and heavy rain that overwhelmed Tribal capacity. All three tribes requested Corps assistance; the Quinault Nation issued a disaster declaration and requested Corps assistance. Three crews provided by the Corps were dispatched over a two-day period to provide technical expertise and assist in the reinforcement of the damaged, existing seawall. The overtopped and damaged seawall was quickly shored up with the addition of 800 tons of riprap rock, and the lower village of Taholah and the risk of flooding to its residents was greatly mitigated.

In 2011 during the Las Conchas Fires, the largest wildfire at that time in the history of New Mexico's, and the Pacheco Fires, the Corps Albuquerque District began emergency response activities at the request of numerous communities, including the Pueblos of Nambe, Santa Clara, San Ildefonso, Cochiti, Santo Domingo, Jemez and Acoma. The Albuquerque District provided both technical and direct assistance under PL 84–99, with particular focus on the most severely impacted Tribal communities, the Pueblos of Santa Clara, Nambe and Cochiti. During the fall of 2011, the Corps developed Technical Assistance Reports identifying increased post-fire flood risk and suggested mitigation for both Santa Clara and Cochiti Pueblos.

In 2012, the Corps responded to assistance requests from numerous communities in New Mexico and Colorado in response to that year's extensive wildfire season, which included the Whitewater-Baldy Complex and Waldo Canyon Fires. The Corps Albuquerque District continued to support both the Nambe and Cochiti Pueblos with individual Technical Assistance Reports and the Santa Clara Pueblo through the Corps Section 203 Tribal Partnership Program.

In 2013, in addition to ongoing and technical support under PL 84–99, the Albuquerque District completed the Technical Assistance Report for the Pueblo of Nambe and initiated Section 205 Small Flood Risk Management Projects with the Pueblos of Santa Clara and Cochiti. Significant flooding occurred across New Mexico in the Fall of 2013 that resulted in numerous assistance requests including, Ohkay Owingeh, the Pueblos of Santa Clara, San Ildefonso, Nambe, Cochiti, Santo Domingo, San Felipe, Santa Ana, Acoma, Zuni, and Isleta, the Navajo Nation including Window Rock, Red Lake Chapter, Gadiiahi, Chinle, Many Farms, and Dilkon Chapters as well as Piute Creek Bridge in Utah. This year, the Corps met with Governor Chavarria from the Pueblo of Santa Clara to explore feasible measures to help mitigate flood risk potential. PL 84–99 Advance Measures funds have been provided to the Corps Albuquerque District to implement physical emergency measures in the near-term, and the district continues to develop longer-term solutions to augment ongoing flood risk reduction efforts. Near-term measures include emergency excavation to create additional stream channel capacity, installation of innovative flood barrier fight products (HESCO bastions), armoring of existing diversion berms and embankments, and the construction of gabion check structures.

In mid-June 2014, the Asaayi Lake Wildfire burned over 14,000 acres, most of which are on the Navajo Nation reservation on the Arizona-New Mexico border. Drainage from the burned area, in the Chuska Mountain watershed, channels into four communities, Sheep Springs, Naschitti, Crystal, and Navajo. Chapters within the Navajo Nation began to experience increased sediment and debris flows almost immediately. The Navajo Nation Department of Emergency Management contacted the Army Corps of Engineers and requested technical assistance. The assistance provided includes modeling and inundation data based on the denuded watersheds, assistance in developing a flood fight plan for the short term (current monsoon season), training in flood fight techniques, and similar measures to help protect lives and property. In addition, the Corps is preparing its own contingency plan to assist the Navajo Nation, if requested, in any future active flood fight activities. The Navajo Nation has also expressed interest in developing a flood risk Continuing Authorities Program project based on the 2013 assessment at Window Rock.

Under the National Disaster Recovery Framework, the Corps and other Federal agencies work together under FEMA direction to respond to a disaster and help in the recovery effort. Tribes with previous experience in disaster response are often better equipped to benefit from the range of available forms of Federal assistance. Tribes facing a catastrophic event for the first time may be quickly overwhelmed by the complex information and the different sources of potential assistance that may be available from the Federal Government. The most effective method to address this concern is targeted outreach, education and training for Tribal governments.

The Corps is making progress in this regard through its cadre of District Tribal Liaisons. The Corps is working to expand Liaison training in USACE emergency response authorities, programs and policies. In addition, the agency is developing appropriate informational material tailored for distribution to tribal governments, and is placing additional emphasis on partnering with Tribal departments of emergency management, including increased use of the Silver Jackets Program. This program is a State- or Tribal-led interagency partnership to coordinate response, recovery and mitigation activities and actions and helps achieve the Corps' goal of flood risk reduction for communities. The Corps has also been coordinating closely with FEMA on interagency cross-training and assignment opportunities to increase the value of the respective Tribal Liaisons resources when facing crisis in Indian Country.

One of the major lessons learned working with Tribal Emergency Response has been the value of the Corps technical assessments and reports Tribes are using assessments and the more detailed Technical Assistance Reports as the basis for applications to other sources of federal and non-federal assistance. Technical Assistance Reports typically include fast-track flood risk analysis, mitigation alternatives evaluation and preferred alternative selection, as well as projected costs for implementation. Their level of detail and organization are being well received, and even requested, as substantive justification for proposal packages.

Mr. Chairman, this concludes my statement of record. Thank you again for the opportunity to provide this statement.

———

RESPONSE TO WRITTEN QUESTIONS SUBMITTED BY HON. JON TESTER TO ELIZABETH ZIMMERMAN

*Question 1.* How are tribes being, or have been engaged, to mold FEMA's Indian policy? Does that process honor the government-to-government relationship?

Answer. FEMA is committed to enhancing its government-to-government relationship with federally recognized Indian tribes. It is in the spirit of this commitment that FEMA developed the Tribal Consultation Policy to implement Executive Order 13175, as a complement the U.S. Department of Homeland Security's Tribal Consultation Policy, to further guide our efforts. Signed by Administrator Fugate on August 12, 2014, the Tribal Consultation Policy provides the guidelines for meaningful, regular, and transparent consultation with tribal officials on FEMA actions that have tribal implications, and enhances FEMA's government-to-government relationship with Indian Country. The policy directly lays out the methods by which FEMA will interact with tribes regarding changes to policies and programs.

FEMA received valuable input from tribes in the development of the Tribal Consultation Policy, consulting with tribes from October 2013 through March 2014. During that time, FEMA presented the policy at conferences, in-person tribal meetings, and listening sessions, and on webinars and conference calls. FEMA received many written comments from tribes, and they are summarized on FEMA's website. FEMA also looked to tribal consultation policies of other agencies, such as the Environmental Protection Agency, to glean best practices and promote consistency in consultation methods and engagement across the Federal Government.

As FEMA implements the Tribal Consultation Policy, its National Tribal Affairs Advisor (NTAA) is meeting with FEMA program offices to highlight the critical elements of the consultation policy and advise programs on the need to engage tribes when undertaking actions that could have tribal implications. FEMA's consultation approach will seek tribal input and provide tribes the opportunity to request consultation earlier in the process of policy and program development. The FEMA Tribal Consultation Policy respects the government-to-government relationship by seeking input from tribes on how and with whom to consult. FEMA seeks to honor tribes as sovereign nations by placing strong emphasis on enabling tribes to guide the methods of consultation.

Additionally, FEMA leadership holds a monthly conference call with the four largest tribal associations—National Congress of American Indians (NCAI), Tribal Emergency Management Agency (iTEMA), National Tribal Emergency Management Council (NTEMC), and United South and Eastern Tribes (USET)—to provide them with program and policy updates. FEMA anticipates that the associations will in turn push out the information to their various members from the 566 federally recognized tribes. This is a useful tool for tribes to learn about potential changes to policies or programs, in addition to being a vehicle for FEMA to provide important information about programs, grants, and policies that could be of use to tribes and tribal officials.

On an operational level, tribes, tribal officials, and tribal associations have been consulted and significantly involved in developing the Tribal Declarations Pilot Guidance. On January 29, 2013, President Obama signed the Sandy Recovery Improvement Act (SRIA) into law. In recognition of the government-to-government relationship, the Act included a provision to provide federally recognized Indian tribal governments the option to request a Presidential emergency or major disaster declaration independent of a state declaration request. In order to allow tribes the choice to use the new authority immediately, FEMA is currently processing tribal declaration requests using the current regulations used for state requests, while at the same time developing declarations procedures specifically for tribal governments that take into account the unique circumstances that affect tribal communities.

As a first step in developing tribal-specific procedures, FEMA developed a first draft of the Tribal Declarations Pilot Guidance, which incorporated initial input from tribal governments that was collected in early 2013. Then, beginning in April 2014, FEMA conducted a second, more in-depth round of consultation with tribal governments through 60 in-person working meetings that occurred throughout the country, attended by more than 500 participants representing more than 200 tribes. During this tribal consultation open comment period, which ended on August 31, FEMA asked tribal governments for their thoughts and comments on a working draft of the Tribal Declarations Pilot Guidance. FEMA is currently adjudicating the comments, and the input will inform the further development of the pilot guidance. FEMA will conduct a second round of consultation before the pilot guidance is finalized. When final, the guidance will describe how FEMA processes and evaluates requests for assistance under the Stafford Act from tribal governments.

*Question 2.* What is FEMA doing to educate and train FEMA field and project officers about tribal nations and sovereignty?

Answer. FEMA created a Tribal Branch within the Office of External Affairs/Intergovernmental Affairs Division as a reflection of the importance of having tribal affairs coordinated under a structure distinct from one that coordinates other governmental stakeholders. This branch is led by FEMA's National Tribal Affairs Advisor and supported by two additional full-time employees working within the branch, which significantly increases the ability of FEMA headquarters to focus on tribal issues.

FEMA regularly looks for opportunities to educate employees. For example, as part of Native American Heritage Month, FEMA hosted an internal event featuring U.S. Department of Agriculture Deputy Under Secretary Arthur "Butch" Blazer, and Bureau of Indian Affairs Director Michael Black. Mr. Blazer and Mr. Black educated FEMA participants about Native Americans' contribution to public service, their experiences as Native Americans in the Federal Government, and their insights on governmental interaction with tribes. This follows FEMA's first agency-wide seminar for Native American Heritage Month in 2013.

During disaster field operations that impact tribal communities, Joint Field Offices offer training for FEMA field and project officers about tribal nations and their unique emergency management needs with regard to tribal culture, tradition, sovereignty, and governance. A regional tribal liaison also deploys to the disaster site to assist both the tribe and FEMA employees who will be working with the tribe.

The Emergency Management Institute (EMI) delivers tribal curriculum courses for tribal officials both online and face-to-face. The tribal curriculum courses are delivered by a team of instructors, some of whom are tribal members themselves, who are carefully selected for their extensive experience working for a tribal government in emergency management. While targeted for tribal audiences, these courses are also often attended by federal employees seeking more in-depth knowledge about tribal emergency management. EMI also offers an online independent study class on Tribal Affairs that is targeted for and open to any current FEMA employees.

FEMA is hosting an ongoing series of Tribal Consultation Policy webinars to educate FEMA employees on how to engage with Indian tribes and tribal officials in regular and meaningful discussion and collaboration on agency actions that have tribal implications.

*Question 3.* The intergovernmental relations between the CCT, DHS/FEMA, and federal agencies needs fine tuning regarding on-reservation funding streams and disaster response. Federal programs established at Rocky Boy's prior to the time of disaster were accessed for short-term emergency response funding. The mechanism needs to be refined to address reimbursement, cost sharing, alternative federal resources, and the interplay with insurance pay-out. How can FEMA's individual assistance program be leveraged to assist tribal members who don't qualify for the public assistance program?

Answer. FEMA recognizes that communities, including tribal nations, face significant and complex challenges after disasters.

FEMA's Individual Assistance Program provides financial assistance to individuals and households that have unmet, disaster-related needs. One program available under Individual Assistance is Individuals and Households Program, which may provide Housing Assistance and/or Other Needs Assistance.

Housing Assistance may include: (1) financial assistance to renters or homeowners for lodging or rental expenses while repairs are made to the pre-disaster primary residence; (2) financial assistance to homeowners to repair disaster-related damage not covered by insurance; and (3) direct temporary housing when disaster survivors cannot make use of financial temporary housing assistance due to a lack of adequate alternate housing. Other Needs Assistance may include (1) financial assistance to pay for disaster-related medical or dental expenses; and (2) financial assistance to pay for expenses incurred for a death due to the disaster.

Public Assistance provides reimbursement to tribal, state, territorial, and local governments and certain private non-profits to repair infrastructure. Public Assistance does not provide financial assistance directly to individuals; and Individual Assistance does not provide assistance to repair infrastructure.

The Stafford Act requires a non-federal cost share for Public Assistance and the Other Needs Assistance provision of Individual Assistance. The Stafford Act does not require a non-federal cost share for temporary housing assistance. It is important to note that the statute prohibits FEMA from duplicating benefits provided by other sources, such as assistance from other Federal agencies or benefits from insurance. FEMA has established a sequence of delivery to provide Public Assistance and Individual Assistance to eligible applicants as expeditiously as possible while not duplicating benefits or services.

FEMA developed a pocket guide to help federally recognized tribes quickly reference information about FEMA programs and how the agency engages with tribes.[1] It also describes disaster assistance provided by other federal agencies, such as the U.S. Small Business Administration (SBA). SBA provides low-interest loans to homeowners, renters, businesses of all sizes, and private, nonprofit organizations that suffered uninsured or underinsured losses from a declared disaster.

FEMA continues to develop tools to assist state, tribal, territorial, and local governments organize and coordinate their own recovery efforts based on the core capabilities outlined in the National Disaster Recovery Framework. If warranted by the needs of the event, tribal governments may request that the Federal Government use the National Disaster Recovery Framework to support the coordination of federal agencies and other sources of recovery assistance, such as non-governmental organizations or state, local, tribal, or territorial governments.

*Question 4.* What strategies are in place, or are being developed, to strengthen the tribal intellectual capacity to successfully administer FEMA's public assistance policy?

---

[1] Pocket guide is available at: *http://www.fema.gov/media-library-data/1414163004909-18662df46f3a3c28f51c1c5b7a209358/FEMA|Pocket|Guide|508|Compliant.pdf*

Answer. The Emergency Management Institute delivers a Tribal Curriculum of courses in a classroom setting for tribal officials, and makes other training available to tribal leaders that is online or face-to-face. The Tribal Curriculum courses are delivered by a team of instructors, the vast majority of whom are tribal members themselves, who are carefully selected for their extensive experience working for a tribal government in emergency management. Based on our admissions records, from the beginning of FY 2011 through mid-July 2014, 1,228 tribal government representatives from 173 different tribes have attended the Tribal Curriculum courses.

Secondly, each FEMA Region with federally recognized tribes has a tribal liaison who works directly with tribes before and after Stafford Act declarations. The tribal liaisons build relationships with tribes and coordinate trainings on Stafford Act programs and processes. As many tribes may not be familiar with disaster assistance programs and related requirements, FEMA is developing tools (such as the recently released *Tribal Pocket Guide*) to help tribal governments better understand FEMA's programs, including the public assistance program.

Finally, FEMA Regions provide hands-on workshops on preparedness, response, recovery, and mitigation that help tribes better understand Stafford Act disaster assistance programs and related requirements. Additionally, Regions provide technical assistance to tribes on continuity of operations plans, emergency operations plans, hazard mitigation plans, and the Threat and Hazard Identification and Risk Assessments process so the tribes will understand their risks, estimate capability requirements, be better prepared for disasters, and be ready to administer disaster assistance.

*Question 5.* What guidance does FEMA need from tribes to develop extensive training and orientation for all new tribal grantees?

Answer. FEMA understands that each tribe is unique and has individualized needs and knowledge levels.

Therefore, to gain further understanding of tribal needs, FEMA's headquarters staff and regional tribal liaisons throughout the country are engaging extensively with tribes. Our regional components engage the tribes with the intent to form lasting relationships that allow candid conversations about education and training needs.

In response to requests from tribes, FEMA is increasingly bringing training courses to the tribes on their lands or in their region (as opposed to bringing tribes to the training), thereby making it more accessible and tailoring it to their needs.

The building of these personal and professional relationships continues to grow from FEMA's increasing tribal engagement, such as the enactment of the Tribal Consultation Policy, the hiring of the National Tribal Affairs Advisor and Tribal Branch staff, and dedication to outreach and engagement. For example, since April 2014, FEMA's National Tribal Affairs Advisor has conducted face-to-face meetings with 24 tribes around the country from Florida to Alaska, and attended six major tribal conferences.

Also at the request of tribes, FEMA is also working with our Grants Program Directorate to provide better technical assistance, educational materials, and engagement opportunities for tribal officials regarding FEMA grant opportunities. By connecting the senior leadership responsible for grants programs directly with tribal officials and tribal national association leadership, FEMA is further distributing important information about funding opportunities and training in Indian Country. FEMA alerts tribes to grant opportunities through advisories and offers guidance through outreach materials.

FEMA Regions provide hands-on workshops on preparedness; response, recovery, and mitigation, and those workshops help tribes better understand Stafford Act disaster assistance programs and related requirements. Additionally, FEMA Regions provide technical assistance to tribes on continuity of operations plans, emergency operations plans, hazard mitigation plans, and the Threat and Hazard Identification and Risk Assessment (THIRA) process so the tribes may be able to understand their risks, estimate capability requirements, be better prepared for disasters, and be ready to administer disaster assistance.

www.ingramcontent.com/pod-product-compliance
Lightning Source LLC
Chambersburg PA
CBHW081141290526

45795CB00006B/2322